HOW OBAMA FAILED BLACK AMERICA

AND HOW TRUMP IS HELPING IT

CLARENCE MCKEE

Palmetto Publishing Group
Charleston, SC

How Obama Failed Black America and How Trump is Helping It
Copyright © 2020 by CLARENCE MCKEE

All rights reserved

First Edition

Printed in the United States

Library of Congress Control Number:2019920579

ISBN-13 978-1-64111-672-5
ISBN-10: 1-64111-672-2

CONTENTS

DEDICATION

This book is dedicated to the millions of black and other Americans with conservative values who all too often dare not speak up due to intimidation, or fear of retribution or retaliation in today's misguided politically correct society.

ACKNOWLEDGMENTS

I want to give special thanks and a note of appreciation to Christopher Ruddy, Chief Executive Officer and Founder of Newsmax Media for bringing me into the Newsmax fold, where I have been able to express my political views to the vast worldwide Newsmax.com audience, both in my Newsmax.com blog, "The Silent Minority" from which many of the articles in this book were taken, and through appearances on Newsmax TV.

Commendation is also due to Newsmax former Opinion Editor Nick Sanchez, whose guidance, encouragement and support has made me a much better writer. The same accolades apply to former editors Paul Scicchitano and David Alliott as well as to the input and advice I receive from Newsmax Information Specialist and editor Anthony Rizzo. In addition, it is also important to acknowledge former Editorial Director Steve Coz—who said, over seven years ago, "Send me an article"—and the great team at Newsmax TV.

Also deserving of mentions and thanks are Christopher Dolan, president and executive Editor of the *Washington Times*, and Human Events Publisher and Editor-in-Chief Will Chamberlain for granting permission to use my articles ("The Closed Minds of Black Leaders," from 1983, and "End Monopoly of Black Overseers," in 2001, respectively) in this book.

Regarding the *Human Events* article, also deserving of a note of appreciation is then-Editor Terry Jeffrey, currently editor-in-chief of CNS News, who published it.

I am honored and flattered that this book was endorsed by former Congressman Lieutenant Colonel Allen B. West (US Army, Retired), Evangelist Alveda King, BlakPAC Chairman George Farrell and former Florida Lieutenant Governor Jennifer Carroll. I thank them all for their support.

Last but not least is the guidance and assistance I received in putting this book together by the great production, design, and editing team at Palmetto Publishing Group—Abby, Erin, Jessica and Jordon.

The political insights in this book result from years of experience and associations with some of the nation's great leaders and public servants, including New York Senator Jacob K. Javits (R-NY); former Federal Communications Commissioner and NAACP Executive Director Benjamin L. Hooks; and, of course, former President Ronald Reagan, during his Reagan for President campaign and presidency—and some of his key staff, including especially Lyn Nofziger, who taught me so much about the world of presidential politics (and who shared a fancy for Tabasco sauce and Bombay gin).

To them and the many others too numerous to mention, in Scottsville, New York; Washington, DC; and Florida, a huge debt of gratitude is owed and expressed.

Finally, none of my accomplishments would have been possible without the support and guidance of my loving parents, "Mac" and Etta McKee!

INTRODUCTION

B arack Obama's greatest legacy and accomplishment was being elected as the first black president of the United States. For black Americans, it went from "Yes, he can" to "No, he didn't."

Barack Obama was a failure in terms of what he and his policies did for black Americans! Yes, there was a certain pride in most black Americans that a black man had been elected president of the United States, when hundreds of years earlier they had suffered through slavery, racism, and blatant racial discrimination in virtually every segment of society and part of the country. Although there has been much progress in race relations, there is still more to be done.

Black Americans, particularly, had high hopes that many of their concerns and issues would be addressed—inferior schools, high unemployment, especially among black youth, violent crime, and gang-terrorized inner cities, to name just a few. Black parents could tell their black children, especially boys, "See what you can become."

White Americans felt and hoped that his election signaled a new "postracial" America. For many whites, especially many in the media, his election gave them a "thrill up the leg," showing that they and the country were not racist. He would bring America, black and white, rich and poor, together. All were duped!

Four years into his presidency, he answered those who felt he could do more for black America, saying in a *Black Enterprise* magazine interview that "I am not the president of Black America; I am the president of the United States of America." [1]

However, he did not hesitate to be president of: gay rights and same-sex marriage America; extreme environmentalists and climate change America;

open borders America; and protect the "dreamers" (children born to illegal immigrants) America!

In 2008 and 2012, blacks gave Obama 95 and 93 percent of their vote, respectively.

Unfortunately, he gave them more symbolism than substance on issues of concern to their communities. Reverend Al Sharpton, Obama's loyal defender, pretty much admitted the symbolic nature of the Obama presidency. In a news clip aired by *Fox News* host Laura Ingraham on April 4 2019 on her show *The Ingraham Angle*, Sharpton, reflecting on the "post-Obama generation," which had seen a "black president and black first family" said: "Now we want to know what it is going to mean. Symbolism is not enough now. It's substance. If there is no substance then we've gotten over the aura of the first." [2]

However, much of black Americans' high hopes for Obama were unfulfilled. Yet there has been little, if any, criticism of his failings in terms of the black community. He remains to this day the darling of the black and white political and civil rights establishments and the mainstream media. His failure to address issues impacting black Americans is the dirty little secret not, or rarely, discussed.

Why?

Not because he is black. It is because he is a black liberal Democrat!

In 2011, when black unemployment exceeded 16 percent, then Congressional Black Caucus (CBC) chairman Rep. Emanuel Cleaver (D-MO) said that members of the CBC "probably would be marching on the White House" if Obama were not president[3]. But they gave him a pass because he was a black liberal Democrat.

Former PBS host Tavis Smiley said in a 2016 interview with the *Huffington Post* that he and others got "so caught that up in the symbolism of the Obama presidency," that they didn't press as hard as they should have on issues that are important to the black community. He went on to say: "Sadly, and it pains me to say this…black folk, in the era of Obama have lost ground in every major economic category…we haven't pressed as hard as we should on the substance of this presidency…Black people and black leaders have been too deferential to this president." [4]

Unlike Smiley, much of the black and white liberal political, academic, and media establishment refused to criticize his failings in terms of the black community—during and after his presidency. They had no such hesitancy in criticizing and often vilifying blacks such as George W. Bush's two black secretaries of state, Condoleezza Rice and Colin Powell, both of whom had also served as his national security advisor—both historic appointments.

President Donald Trump, whose policies have brought the black unemployment rate to its lowest numbers in history, receives no credit for this achievement from these establishments!

This book is not intended to be an exhaustive treatise on President Barack Obama's disappointing record on many issues impacting black America, including the affordable housing crisis and growing homelessness, violence in our inner cities, and other areas. Rather, its purpose is to illustrate the failure of the "First Black President" to address some of the key issues facing black America and show how the policies of President Donald Trump on those issues are helping black Americans.

The book is composed of over thirty of the nearly two hundred articles I have written for my "Silent Minority Blog" at Newsmax.com as well as additional essays and commentary.[5]

Part I, "How Obama Failed Black America," is composed of articles discussing Barack Obama's failure to address the problems and needs of the nation's black community in a variety of areas. The selected articles outline how the "First Black President" failed to step up to the plate and generally ignored the plight of blacks on issues, including unemployment and the economy, crime and prison reform, and the political and negative impact of illegal immigration on blacks.

Rather, he seemed insensitive to such issues and gave priority to addressing concerns of other groups, including those who favor same-sex marriage, abortion on demand, and amnesty for illegal aliens. When it suited his purpose, he maintained his relevance to blacks by wrapping himself in his own "blackness" and, with his first attorney general, exploited the race card when it suited his purpose. Remember when he said: "If I had a son, he'd look like Trayvon" referring to Trayvon Martin, the seventeen-year-old black youth slain by white security guard George Zimmerman in Florida.

Demonizing the police and fostering racial division was a method to show relevancy to blacks—and they fell for it!

Part II, "How Trump Is Helping Black America," discusses how Obama turned his back on blacks and how Trump is helping the black community on illegal immigration, criminal justice reform with the First Step Act, abortion and sanctity of life, school choice and vouchers for inner city students, and urban revitalization and Opportunity Zones, as well as how his economy is benefiting black Americans.

Part III, "Epilogue," expresses a consistent theme in many of my *Newsmax* articles in this book on how the black political and civil rights leadership has historically failed the black community by being an echo chamber for the Democratic Party and the liberal establishment on virtually all issues. It shows that this is not a recent phenomenon and was the subject of my first published article in 1983 in the *Washington Times*, "The closed minds of black Leaders," and a subsequent article in *Human Events Online* in 2001, "End Monopoly of Black Overseers." Both illustrate that not much has changed since 1983. Unlike other voter groups, blacks are still in the "hip pocket" and taken for granted by the Democratic Party counting on black leaders and politicians to continue to act as "overseers" of the "Black Democrat Plantation."

ORGANIZATION

The articles in this book are grouped by subject matter in the respective chapters. Each article includes the original headline with the date of publication in case anyone wishes to consult the original article. In most cases, the articles are in chronological order because the sequence was determined by and related to real-time events which are the subject of the articles. Accompanying photographs, which were included in the headline portion of the articles, have been excluded.

Since these were all published in Newsmax.com, it was unnecessary to write "Newsmax" at the beginning or end of each article. Also omitted is the biographical information that originally appeared at the conclusion of each article.

—Clarence McKee

PART I:

HOW OBAMA
FAILED
BLACK AMERICA

CHAPTER 1
IMMIGRATION AND OPEN BORDERS

Obama Brings Illegals Over — at All Costs
Monday, June 16, 2014 07:26 AM

Remember when celebrated black American Nobel and Pulitzer Prize-winning novelist Toni Morrison, for whatever reason, called Bill Clinton "the first black president?"

Some might argue that Barack Obama, in addition to being the first black president, may also be remembered as the "first Hispanic president."

Why?

He is doing all that he can to assist mostly illegal Hispanic immigrants to enter our nation virtually unchecked and ultimately significantly increase the political power of the Hispanic population. Being black and not Hispanic, he can do it better than if he were Hispanic because he will not be accused of being "partial" to his own ethnic group.

Just as he seems to avoid being accused of doing too much for blacks and not being "president of black America," he can wrap himself around the open borders support for "dreamers" and not be accused of appearing to be partial to his own as an Hispanic president would be for doing the same.

In so many words, Obama is doing for the Central and South American Hispanic/Latino populations wanting to come to America what Lyndon Johnson did for blacks in America with the Civil Rights and Voting Rights Acts.

In this case, it is the "right" to get to the United States illegally without consequences.

His policies on immigration have encouraged thousands of illegal, undocumented to be politically correct, mostly Hispanic immigrants to cross our borders.

It will lead to the increased political power for Hispanics in state, local, and national elections, assuming they register and turnout to vote after becoming citizens. Or, if not citizens, they manage to take advantage of weakened or non-existent state voter identification laws which Obama's Justice Department is attempting to nullify.

Either way, it will be mean a dilution of black voter power and the defeat of black politicians whose urban districts become more Hispanic.

Two years ago, Obama relaxed deportation rules on illegal minors. Now we have thousands of so-called "refugees" pouring into the United States by the busload from Central America with God only knows how many gang members, potential terrorists or communicable disease infiltrated "plants" among them lured by Obama's humanitarian generosity.

As Newsmax's Tod Beamon recently reported in Newsmax.com, the Obama administration estimates that 60,000 children under 18 will enter the U.S. illegally alone this year. It's expected to grow to nearly 130,000 next year.

Is anyone thinking about their safety and welfare? How are they to adjust in a strange land with no parents to protect and nurture them? Do you really think the Department of Health and Human Services will be a good "mommy and daddy" or "big brother or sister"?

Don't kid yourself. They can't even manage Obamacare for Americans! Who will pay for their education, healthcare and housing? You guessed it. American taxpayers!

And, according to an article a year ago by Eric Rodriguez, vice president, office of Research, Advocacy and Legislation of the National Council of La Raza, there is "an already rich pool of Latino citizens not yet registered, between now and 2028, nearly 900,000 Latino citizens will turn 18 every year."

His article went on to point out that there are about 11.1 million eligible but unregistered Hispanics and more than 2.5 million registered Hispanics didn't vote in 2012. He concludes by saying: "it is indisputable that the Latino electorate is larger and more powerful than at any point in history and is poised to exercise its power more than ever before."

Did Congress set this in motion?

No!

Under Obama's Executive Order in 2012, young people who would be eligible can receive work permits and protection from deportation for two years, with the possibility of renewal. It is estimated that this will impact a minimum of 800,000 people.

Black — and white — Democrat elected officials in congressional, state and local districts in California, Florida, New York and elsewhere will soon see that the Obama influx of Hispanic voters will dilute their black and white voter bases against Hispanic challengers in districts with significant Hispanic voters.

Just ask Congressman Charlie Rangel, D-N.Y., who narrowly defeated a Hispanic opponent in 2012 and who is in a tough fight seeking to defeat the same opponent in November in a district that has become increasingly more Latino. I believe he will lose.

So, Hispanics really can say that, for what his immigration policies have accomplished, Obama is the "first Hispanic president."

His legacy to Hispanics: growing political power through open borders!

His legacy to blacks: growing political power to Hispanics through open borders!

As Charles Cherry, Publisher of the Florida Courier, Florida's only statewide black newspaper recently wrote: "Being the 'first black' to hold political office has played out.

Rather a White/Hispanic person who would advocate for our interests than a black person who would warm the seat. Where's an "unbought and embossed" Shirley Chisholm when you need her?"

The Obama Legacy Spirals Downward
Monday, July 14, 2014 10:22 AM

It was really embarrassing: The president of the United States, in shirt sleeves, laughing and joking, telling an audience in Austin, Texas, that "I'm just telling the truth now, I don't have to run for office again."

The question is Mr. President: What were you not telling us the truth about in 2008 and 2012?

We now know that "You can keep your doctor" and "You can keep your healthcare plan" were not true statements.

And remember this one: "transparency and the rule of law will be the touchstones of this presidency?"

What else did we miss?

It's no wonder that a recent poll rated Obama the worst president since World War II.

Why?

While Obama was making jokes in Austin, drinking beer and playing pool in Colorado, thousands of illegal immigrant children were languishing in makeshift warehouses and processing centers on our Texas border and elsewhere with Air Force One a few short minutes flying time away.

He could have taken the initiative and accepted Texas Governor Rick Perry's invitation to visit the border facilities overrun with these children.

He did not!

He could have been a leader and co-opted his adversaries by going to the border not only to thank the caregivers, but also to deliver a harsh message to those sending and permitting the passage of these children to the United States.

He did not. He was MIA — missing in action!

After all, how would Obama explain going to the border to view firsthand the immigration crisis when he has not seen fit to visit his own hometown of Chicago in the midst of its own crisis: an epidemic of violence where over 3,000 have been shot since 2013 including this year's bloody Fourth of July weekend where 82 people were shot and 16 killed.

In large measure, the border crisis is of Obama's own making. It was his "Dreamer" executive order ending deportations of illegal immigrants who entered the country as children with their parents that has led to this tidal wave of children.

Throughout Central America, the word went out: "Send us your children; we will take care of them."And they did!

And we will!

So, what is the president's solution to this problem that he in large part created?

He now wants Congress to give him nearly 4 billion dollars to do just that — take care of the thousands of illegal children including paying for their education, healthcare, and lawyers — not stop the influx or beef up border security.But there is growing pushback.

As one Houston black housewife said in a recent television interview, "What about our kids in our neighborhoods?"

Even the Rev. Jesse Jackson was forced to say that, while we needed to help those on the border, "We can't turn our backs on our children at home, either."

In many ways, the border crisis is fast becoming another Obama scandal to be added to an already crowded list:

- The Veterans Administration

- The IRS

- Fast and Furious

- Benghazi

- Trading a suspected army deserter for five high-level terrorists while heroic Marine Sergeant Andrew Tahmooressi languishes in a Mexican jail

- Being accused of stifling the free expression of information and transparency by 38 news organizations

- Sending "pink slips" to soldiers, many of whom are still in combat in Afghanistan.

In addition to the above, the Obama administration has been on the losing side of over a dozen U.S. Supreme Court unanimous decisions against its efforts to expand the reach and power of the executive branch of the federal government. Look for more judicial defeats to come regarding the administration's unilateral changes to Obamacare.

If all of this were not enough of an indictment of a failed presidency, keep in mind that there could be many more troubles for Obama if it is discovered that his already secretive government is hiding the truth — lying — about the true potential for a public health crisis because of diseases these children and the expected 90,000 more by September — aided by drug cartels, human traffickers, and coyote smugglers — could expose our own children to: tuberculosis, chicken pox, swine flu, and scabies.

And lest we forget, how many of these older illegals are sent by design by our enemies to one day play terroristic havoc in one more of our cities — remember Boston?

When elected, hopes were high — especially among most blacks, the liberal left, and media — that Obama would do great things for the country at home and abroad and heal old wounds and divisions. He was supposed to unite, not divide, the country.

Instead, he and his minions have made racial and class warfare an art form — criticize him and his policies and you are a racist, a homophobe, anti-woman, against the middle class or worse.

And so, given this picture, it is not looking good for the legacy of the "first black" president.

If he, and those who think they are serving him, continue the current pace of scandal, incompetence, and lack of leadership, history may rate him as one of the worst presidents — and not just since World War II!

Blacks Big Losers in Border Crisis

Wednesday, July 23, 2014 12:48 PM

"The interests of black Americans are clear: No amnesty, no guest workers, enforce the immigration laws." So said T. Willard Fair, President and CEO of the Urban League of Greater Miami, past Chairman of the Florida State Board of Education, and Board member of the Center for Immigration Studies.

Was Fair reacting to the current border crisis? No.

He was speaking to a Congressional Committee seven years ago on the impact of mass immigration policies on black communities: "scholars estimate that immigration is the reason for one-third of the drop in employment among black men, and even some of the increase in incarceration."

He posed questions as valid today as then: Which is more likely to help an ex-convict or recovering addict get hired at an entry-level job and start the climb back to a decent life — amnesty and more immigration, or enforcement and less immigration?

Which is more likely to persuade a teenager in the inner city to reject the lure of gang life and instead stick with honest employment — amnesty and more immigration, or enforcement and less immigration?

Historically, Fair is not alone in his concern over the impact of immigration on black Americans.

Titans of black history such as Frederick Douglass, Booker T. Washington, and A. Phillip Randolph all raised concerns.

As Douglass, the black journalist and former slave wrote in 1853: "The old avocations, by which colored men obtained a livelihood, are rapidly, unceasingly and inevitably passing into other hands . . . Every hour sees the black man elbowed out of employment by some newly arrived emigrant, whose hunger and whose color are thought to give him a better title to the place. "

Fair's and Douglass' comments are particularly appropriate in light of the current border crisis due in no small measure to the "Y'all come" message of Obama's immigration policies.

As black writer Patricia L. Dickson wrote last month in American Thinker: "It appears that President Obama and the Democrat Party are willing to throw Black Americans overboard in exchange for amnesty. In a quest to maintain power, the Democrats have discovered that there are not enough black American voters to keep them in office."

Forward thinking blacks have been sounding the alarm that blacks are and will be the real losers, not only in the this border crisis, but in the immigration battles ahead.

Last year, several black leaders, including Fair, warned Congress of the harm that the "Gang of Eight" immigration bill would inflict upon black workers: "We are asking that you oppose Senate Bill S.744 because of the dramatic effect it will have on the availability of employment for African American workers."

Frank Morris, former executive director of the Congressional Black Caucus Foundation, said: "Increasing immigration levels . . . will flood labor markets with millions more people, leading to higher unemployment, more poverty, and a lower standard of living for many in the black community."

More recently, in an eight page letter May 20 to the Chair of the Congressional Black Caucus, U.S. Civil Rights Commissioner Peter Kirsanow, a black Republican, said in part: "it is likely that if illegal immigrants are granted legal status, more people will come to America illegally and will further crowd African-American men (and other low-skilled men and women) out of the workforce . . . Giving amnesty to illegal immigrants would only exacerbate this problem facing low-skilled men, who are disproportionately African-American."

As usual, the Congressional Black Caucus and NAACP are leading from behind and on the wrong side — against the interests of their own constituents.

The Caucus is in favor of amnesty for illegals.

Why? Political self-preservation.

Most of them come from majority-black districts which are becoming increasingly Hispanic putting their futures at risk — just ask Congressman Charles Rangel, D-N.Y., who almost lost his seat to a Hispanic.

As to the NAACP, its former president, Benjamin Todd Jealous, was the keynote speaker at the pro-amnesty rally in Washington, D.C. last year. This is the same Jealous who admitted on "Meet the Press" that black Americans "are doing far worse" than when President Obama first took office.

It's no wonder that Hispanics have taken the place of blacks as the most coveted — and politically respected — of all minority groups. While blacks are locked at the hip to the Democratic Party and are its most loyal voting block — for which they got nothing from Obama — Hispanics are willing to take a look at both sides and ask "what do we get in return"?

They can boast of two governors, both Republican; three U.S. Senators, two of whom are Republican and scores of state legislators many of whom are Republicans — and whom Hispanics respect. Blacks have only one Republican U.S. Senator — Tim Scott of South Carolina — whom black leaders disrespect at every opportunity.

So it is understandable that Hispanics are more politically valued than blacks — even by the black president — just look at which constituencies he caters to!

The caucus, NAACP and others in the black Democratic liberal establishment will not heed the warnings of Fair, Douglas, Commissioner Kirsanow and others and look out for their constituents' interests.

To again quote Ms. Dickinson: "If black Americans are willing to continue to support the president to their own detriment, their psychosis is worse than I thought."

Obama's Amnesty Pushes Blacks Aside

Monday, November 17, 2014 09:41 AM

Talk about back stabbing!

It looks like Barack Obama is going to give a pre-Thanksgiving gift — some would say "knife in the back" — to black America: virtual amnesty for nearly 5 million illegal aliens.

Those getting amnesty will be happy. Blacks should not be.

Nationally, black unemployment is 11 percent and for those 16-24, it exceeds 21 percent. If this were not bad enough, in the president's home town of Chicago, the Chicago Urban League reported last January that an alarming 92 percent of black male teenagers didn't have a job.

You would think that Obama would be moving heaven and earth during the last two years of his term to develop a "10-part jobs plan" to bring those numbers down for his most loyal constituency.

No!

His payback for their support is an expected "10-part immigration plan" giving virtual amnesty to millions of illegals — at their expense.

Preliminary reports say that key parts of the plan include protecting up to 5 million illegals from deportation, providing many with work permits, allowing many parents of children who are American citizens of legal residents to obtain legal work documents and expanding opportunities for legal immigrants who have high-tech skills.

"Work permits." "Work documents." "High-tech skills." Such opportunities for employment must sound good to unemployed Americans.

How about working to expand opportunities and training for the 11 percent of unemployed black adults and 22 percent black youth so they can get those "high tech skills," Mr. President?

If blacks were disappointed over Obama and the Democrats ignoring their problems and catering to the demands of every other group before the midterm elections, they should really feel like abandoned stepchildren after this program is officially announced.

Just think, even illegal aliens are moved ahead of blacks to the front of Obama's bus.

If Obamacare consultant Jonathan Gruber thinks American voters are stupid, just imagine what he and the liberal Democratic elites think of their most loyal supporters who give all to the party and demand nothing in return. Their reward: amnesty for illegals.

While black Americans' ancestors came to this country in chains and shed blood and suffered vicious racism and discrimination for centuries in the fight for the rights of citizenship, Obama is giving those who came here illegally the same benefits with a swipe of a pen.I guess you could call it "Obama's Emancipation Proclamation for illegal aliens."

While thousands of black men and women languish in jails and prisons for various drug and other non-violent offenses, how many illegals who have committed more serious crimes will get an Obama "no deportation pass?"

If you think the unemployment status of blacks is bad now, just wait until "Obama's millions" get legal status. Thousands more will pour across the border to "Obama's promise land" to crowd the low-skilled job market and compete for job and educational opportunities as well as healthcare and social services benefits.

The question is: Who will speak up for black Americans?

Dedrick Asante-Muhammad, senior director of NAACP's economic department, said the unemployment rate among minorities must be addressed:

"The 2-to-1 employment disparity between African Americans and whites is not closing and appears to be a permanent part of the economy . . . This disparity, as well as the disparity found in Latino unemployment, must be addressed."

Well said!

But, don't think for a moment that his bosses at the NAACP will dare say or do anything that criticizes Barack Obama's bringing in 5 million people to compete with black and Hispanic Americans who are direly in need of jobs.

The NAACP has become front-row cheerleaders in Obama's and the Democratic Party's "Amen Corner." It will rubber stamp anything he does or says — regardless of its impact on black Americans in whose best interests the NAACP is supposed to act.

What about the Congressional Black Caucus?

Same thing — totally in the bag for Obama with most dancing to whatever tune he, the Democratic Party, Harry Reid, or Nancy Pelosi play — amnesty included.

Al Sharpton and Jesse Jackson? Don't even ask!

The real irony is that the it will be a Republican Congress that offers any hope to black Americans that Obama's rush to add up to 5 million competitors for their jobs and educational opportunities may be stalled.

And that includes the three newly elected black Republican members of the Senate and House — the three people that the NAACP and the Democratic liberal establishment love to hate: U.S. Senator Tim Scott of South Carolina,

Congressman-elect Will Hurd of Texas, and Congresswoman-elect Mia Love of Utah.

How sweet it is.

CHAPTER 2

THE ECONOMY
AND JOBS

Obama's Food Stamp Nation

Friday, August 3, 2012 04:08 PM

Newt was right — Barack Obama is the "Food stamp president." He's turning America into the "Food Stamp Nation."

How bad is it?

A new Heritage Foundation Report, "Reforming the Food Stamp Program," by Robert Rector and Katherine Bradley says it all.

Referring to the nearly doubling of combined federal and state food stamp spending between 2000 and 2007, it states that Obama has "more than doubled spending on food stamps again. Spending rose from $39 billion in 2008 to a projected $85 billion in 2012." It also states that he "plans to spend nearly $800 billion on food stamps in the next decade."

Two years ago Heritage pointed out that Obama's stimulus package in 2009 expanded eligibility and, because of rising unemployment, suspended the provision that "required able-bodied recipients without children to work at least half-time."

The report also shatters the misconception that food stamps are short term: ". . . at any given moment, the majority of recipients will become long-term dependents . . . Historically, half of food stamp aid to families with children has gone to families that have received aid for 8.5 years or more."

The program "discourages work, rewards idleness, and promotes long-term dependence." Instead of being an "open-ended entitlement" program that gives "one-way handouts," the report recommends conversion to a "work activation program." Under this concept, when the economy improves, "able-bodied non- elderly adults . . . should be required to work, prepare for work, or at least look for work as a condition of receiving aid."

I agree.

I would also require recipients to "put some skin in the game." Historically, most recipients put up a certain amount based on their household income in return for a stamp allotment of much greater value.

To those who think I am being cold and uncaring. Not true!

Three of the most rewarding years of my life were spent working on improving the food stamp program. In 1969, the U.S. Senate Select Committee on Nutrition and Human Needs was investigating hunger and malnutrition in the United States and what changes should be made in domestic food programs to meet the needs of the poor.

Food stamps in some form had been around since the Depression era. The program became permanent in 1964. The main food assistance program had been the "Commodity Distribution Program" which provided surplus agriculture foods to the needy. Food stamps allowed recipients to purchase perishable products.

The Committee was chaired by Sen. George McGovern, D-S.D. Jacob K. Javits, R-N.Y., the ranking Republican, appointed me to be the staff member for the Republicans.

In addition to McGovern, Democrats included Allen Ellender, D-La., Herman Talmadge, D-Ga., and Walter Mondale, D-Minn.

Republican Members included Marlow Cook, D-Ky., and Robert Dole, R-Kan. One noteworthy point, Marlow Cook's staff member assigned to the committee was a young man named Mitch McConnell, the current Senate Minority Leader. Peter Dominick, R-Colo., was later replaced by Ed Gurney, R-Fla., who had just made history by defeating Florida Governor LeRoy Collins making him the first Republican elected to the U.S. Senate since Reconstruction.

We conducted hearings in different parts of the country including migrant camps in Immokalee and Fort Myers, Fla. and saw obviously malnourished children. In Immokalee, Ellender asked one black woman holding her baby "are you married?" She said "yes sir." I know he was hoping for a "no."

In Fort Myers, we were met by then Gov. Claude Kirk, the first Florida Republican governor since Reconstruction. His message: Florida was taking care of its poor folks. Javits lit into him! Years later, I got to know the governor and often kidded him about the encounter.

I accompanied Javits to the White House where he urged President Nixon to revamp food and child nutrition programs and not let McGovern take the lead. During that period, I also had frequent meetings with Nixon's assistant Agriculture Secretary Richard Lyng — who later became Agriculture Secretary under Ronald Reagan —over reforms that the administration could make on its own.

In May of 1969, the Food and Nutrition Service was formed in the Department of Agriculture to coordinate child and adult food programs.

In December, Nixon held a White House conference on food, nutrition, and health to which I was a consultant.

When McGovern introduced his own "Hunger Bill," I told Javits he should not sign on but do his own bill. On Aug. 6, 1969, he introduced S.2769 — the Health, Nutrition and Human Needs Act of 1969." In addition to food stamp reform, the bill also included nutrition education requirements and child nutrition reforms including national standards for free and reduced price lunches.

Many of the food stamps provisions became law in early 1971 in Public Law 91- 671.

Where are we now?

Congressman Marlin Stutzman, R-Ind., recently pointed out in a Wall Street Journal article co-authored by Michael Needham of Heritage Action for America the following:

"In the 1970's, just one in 50 Americans received food benefits. Today that number is one in seven. In other words, 15 percent of the U.S. population is dependent on food stamps."

Even though the program is now called the "Supplemental Nutrition Assistance Program (SNAP) — probably to lessen the "welfare "stigma to the expanding army of recipients — the result is the same:

We are a "Food Stamp Nation!"

Food for votes anyone?

Why the Black Silence on Unemployment?

Thursday, April 18, 2013 03:39 PM

One thing is sure about President Barack Obama's legacy. When black leaders express outrage and march to protest high black unemployment rates under a future white president and administration, the answer should be: "Wait a minute. You didn't go after Obama for 14 percent black unemployment rates, so don't come after me."

The average black unemployment rate for February and March stood at 13.5 percent. Economist Walter E. Williams states that black youth unemployment is more than 40 percent nationally and in some cities unemployment of black working-age males is more than 50 percent.

Yet, we have heard no real expressions of outrage or condemnation of Obama for the plight of blacks by the NAACP, Congressional Black Caucus (CBC), or the other usual suspects who would be all over a Republican, or even a white Democratic president with such deplorable numbers.

The National Urban League's State of Black America report for 2013 released this month states that, notwithstanding social and economic gains, the African-American equality gap with whites has changed little since the 1963 March on Washington for Jobs and Freedom 50 years ago. The League's senior vice president said that the report "underscores that employment remains the biggest barrier to equality in our country . . ."

So why the silence?

The reason was given two months before the election.

Then CBC Chairman Emanuel Cleaver was widely quoted saying that, "if we had a white president, we'd be marching around the White House . . . the president knows we are going to act in deference to him in a way we wouldn't to someone white."

Mr. Cleaver and the other silent black leaders think they can give Obama a pass and then try to hold a white president's feet to the fire and make demands when Obama is long gone.

As so-called leaders looking out for their black flock, they have blown their credibility.

Maybe they should take a page out of the book of Detroit City Councilwoman JoAnn Watson who said that Obama should "bring home the bacon . . . Our people in an overwhelming way supported the re-election of this president and there ought to be a quid pro quo . . ."

But, on the other hand, why should they complain now? After all, blacks gave Obama 93 percent of their vote and a recent poll suggests that blacks may not be too concerned.

According to a February Zogby on-line poll of 1,002 black Americans commissioned by Bob Johnson, BET founder and Chairman of the RLJ Companies:

- 91 percent had a favorable opinion of Obama

- 72 percent said his election helped "in the lives of most African-Americans"

- 30 percent said their personal finances "are better off now than they were four years ago and 48 percent said they are "about the same"

- 44 percent felt that blacks are "about the same "as they were four years ago" while 25 percent say they are "better off"

Unbelievable!

So, what or who is at fault for a black unemployment rate twice that for whites?

Based on the survey results, it is not Obama's failed economic policies. Fifty percent believed that it was caused by the failure of the "education system for minorities/African Americans; while only 25 percent blamed lack of "good government policies."

As Mr. Johnson told a National Press Club audience recently, this country "would never tolerate white unemployment at 14 and 15 percent" and that no one "would ever stay in office at such rates."

Well, blacks obviously have no problem with it as long as it is coming from a liberal black Democratic president. Blacks didn't ask for anything or get anything in return for the 93 percent support — Hispanics and the gay rights community, on the other hand, got some "bacon" — they demanded it.

Selective outrage seems to be reserved for Republicans, black or white, who advocate alternative policies and options for dealing with unemployment and other problems impacting urban America.

As more and more African Americans careen to the back of the economic bus, the sound of silence is deafening, disturbing, and disgraceful from Obama's fellow "black elite" so-called leaders on his inability to get the economy going and his lack of attention to the plight of his black "brothers and sisters." They delivered votes for him, but his economy has not delivered jobs for them as they teeter on the edge of the economic cliff.

As to expressions of outrage, speeches, and marches to the White House demanding action, don't count on it as long as "Bro Prez" is in the White House.

To be fair, Congresswoman Maxine Waters of the CBC was a lonely voice over two years ago: "We want to give him every opportunity, but our people are hurting. The unemployment is unconscionable. We don't know what the strategy is."

The same applies today more than ever. Where are those in the black leadership who have the courage to echo Ms. Waters' criticism today?

Let me predict what will happen if a Republican return to the White House in 2016 — or even a white Democrat. You can be sure that that all hell will break loose if he or she fails to help inner cities and the struggling middle black class within the first 100 days in office. That is if there is any black middle class left after eight years of "Obamanomics."

Obama Can Do Much More for African Americans
Friday, August 30, 2013 10:52 PM

Are we all feeling good and patting ourselves on the back?

The celebration and speeches of the 50th anniversary of the 1963 March on Washington have come and gone.

Since there was very little from the 2013 March that will be memorialized 50 years from now, it might be a good time to reflect on where we really are in terms of Dr. King's "dream" of equality, racial harmony, justice and his call to "Let freedom ring."

Of course things have changed for the better in America on the racial front. After all, we have a black president of the United States and attorney general; we have had two black secretaries of state and national security advisers; scores of black elected officials and judges at the local, state and federal level; and blacks assuming positions of power in corporate America.

Are there strides still to be made?

Of course, there are.

As to race relations, things have seen progress. In fact, a recent Rasmussen poll found that 69 percent of likely voters think race relations are better today than they were 50 years ago when King gave his famous "I Have a Dream" speech.

This seems to be a perfect tribute on the 50th anniversary.

But wait!

Let's take a closer look at reality.

In that same poll, nearly 90 percent say race relations have gotten worse or remained about the same since the election of the nation's first black president.

So, what's the problem?

We have a president whose skin is black — the same as Dr. King's. But, in terms of working to help the poor as Dr. King did, skin color is about all that King and Obama have in common.

One would think that the first black president would be an advocate for black children trapped in underperforming urban schools; that he would be supportive of vouchers so they and their parents can have the same choice for educational excellence as he does for his daughters.

One would think that he and his black attorney general would want to "let freedom ring" for such children.

Not quite.

As if killing a popular voucher program for low income students in the District of Columbia was not enough, we now learn that he and his attorney general are going after the state of Louisiana in an effort to kill that state's voucher program which benefits mostly poor black children.

No letting "freedom ring" for their educational benefit.

While King's drummer was his God, conscience and helping the poor, Obama marches to the drumbeat of teachers' unions — poor black children's education is not in the band,

King and his associates, such as former U. N. Ambassador, Congressman and Atlanta Mayor Andrew Young, sought to build bridges and have allies among whites and politicians of both parties. Obama, his attorney general and their allies in the "civil rights establishment" have become masters at racial divisiveness and race baiting.

To the Obama cheering squad, the only crimes are those committed against blacks by whites. Those by blacks against blacks or blacks against whites are not worthy of condemnation. Not quite a tribute to Dr. King.

The answer to the question of why things have changed is simple.

King was from — and answered to the black masses. Obama is from and answers to the black and white liberal elite.

In King's day, his support came mostly from blacks: lawyers, churches, newspaper publishers, owners of segregated restaurants and hotels in Atlanta, Birmingham, Washington, D.C., and Memphis, to name a few. Many sympathetic whites helped and sacrificed as well.

Today, much of the money and support going to the major civil rights groups, many black politicians (and the Jacksons and Sharpton's) is not from black people. You guessed it — unions and the liberal Democratic Party establishment.

Just check out the District of Columbia City Council's vote against bringing Walmart and jobs into economically depressed black areas of the nation's capital.

I think I know whose side King would have taken. Unlike those — like former Mayor Marion Barry — who supported unions over Walmart, he would not have put union interests above those of poor black residents who needed jobs.

I guess he and others in union pockets did not want D.C. inner city residents to be "free at last" in their quest for neighborhood grocery shopping and jobs.

Of course, Obama was silent. After all, it was a local issue.

Finally, Obama as a black president could do so much from his bully pulpit. He could speak out on issues so important to the black community 50 years later — more than 70 percent out-of-wedlock births, the foul language gangsta rap of his entertainment industry friends, fathers not marrying the mothers of their children, baggy pants prison-like wardrobes, cover to cover tattoos that don't enhance job prospects, and the need to be articulate and speak English as did Dr. King and the president himself not to mention the crisis of young black male incarceration and drop-out rates.

These are some of the issues that we still have to "overcome" 50 years after the March on Washington, issues that are inhibiting many blacks from enjoying the fruits of Dr. King's labor.

It's too bad the first black president won't step up to the plate.

The Real State of Obama's Union

Monday, January 27, 2014 10:30 AM

No matter what President Obama says in his official sixth State of the Union address, the real state of "Obama's union" is not good.

Given his recent New Yorker interview where he stated that there's ". . . some folks who just really dislike me because they don't like the idea of a black president," one could argue that any problems with the State of Obama's Union are either race based or due to Fox News or Rush Limbaugh whom he also faulted for his problems.

For nearly six years, Obama has remained silent while his supporters in the mainstream media and the black and white liberal establishments played the race card, accusing anyone opposing his policies of being racists or sellouts.

Such comments make the president appear to be a whiner not realizing that his unpopularity is based on his policies and lack of leadership and not race, Limbaugh, or Fox News. They are beneath the Office of President of the United States.

As he enters the far turn of his presidency hobbled with record-low poll numbers, it is not inconceivable that he will barely limp across the finish line — especially if he loses his Democratic Senate in November.

Other than his race, will history remember his presidency for any outstanding accomplishments — other than killing Osama bin Laden?

It will record that the president who says that racism contributed to his falling poll numbers averaged 41 percent of the white vote in his two election victories.

It will also note that he received slam-dunk majorities of Asian, black, and Hispanic voters thanks in no small way to the insensitivities and failings of his Republican opponents and their campaigns.

They failed miserably to recognize, respect, and show empathy for these key voter groups and their issues. Whether the same political stupidity will be repeated in key November Senate races is yet to be seen.

If the GOP has not designed an Asian, black, and Hispanic voter strategy for key Senate races for 2014 by now, they are sending the same "we do not want or need you" losing message.

So, what is the state of Obama's union?

According to recent polls, 62 percent of voters say they dislike his policies. His disapproval rating is 53 percent with 59 percent of voters opposing his flagship program Obamacare including 30 percent of Democrats and 53 percent of Independents. And, a Bloomberg National Poll last month showed that 58 percent of Americans disapproved of his economic leadership.

History will show that these bad numbers are not due to his race, Fox News, or Rush Limbaugh.

They are due to his failed policies such as Obamacare, a still-struggling economy as well as the lingering cloud of dishonesty and abuse of power hovering over him and his administration.

Obama's union is defined by scandals such as the IRS' almost unprecedented abuse of power to punish his and Democrats' political enemies; outright lies on Obamacare; initial deception regarding the NSA's collection of data on American citizens; the apparent deception and cover-up on Benghazi and Fast and Furious; the failure to take responsibility or demand accountability; remaining detached, disengaged, uninformed and appearing to be oblivious to anything going on in his own administration; fostering class warfare by pitting the rich against the poor and middle class; and, selective enforcement of the laws.

A few more gems of the state of Obama's union, as related to blacks, were highlighted in a recent excellent Newsmax.com article by Jennifer G. Hickey:

- Black Americans have overwhelmingly supported Barack Obama in two presidential elections, but they have fallen further behind during his term in office, losing ground in measures of income, employment, and education.

- The national unemployment rate has dropped to 7 percent, but the jobless rate for blacks has hardly moved since Obama took office, declining from 12.7 percent in 2009 to 12.5 percent.

- The poverty rate for blacks sharply increased, rising from 12 percent in 2008 to 16.1 percent. Median income declined by 3.6 percent for white households to $58,000, but fell 10.9 percent to $33,500 for black households.

The article quoted Harry Alford, president of the National Black Chamber of Commerce, saying that "we are worse off than we were when he came into office."

So, the state of Obama's union is rather clear based on all of all of the above, and much more not cited, for all Americans.

For Obama's most loyal supporters, for whom he claims to have a racial umbilical link, the real state of Obama's union for black Americans was summed up by PBS's Travis Smiley:

"The data are going to indicate sadly that when the Obama administration is over, black people will have lost ground in every single leading economic indicator category. On that regard the president ought to be held responsible."

So much for the reality of the "state of Obama's union."

Just how close his official State of the Union address reflects reality remains to be seen.

———————————————

Obama's Failed Black Legacy
Tuesday, January 17, 2017 12:47 PM

Barack Obama's greatest legacy and accomplishment was being elected as the first black president of the United States.

For black Americans, it has been downhill ever since, from "Yes we can" to "No he didn't."

Yes, there was a certain pride in all black Americans that a black man had been elected President of the United States, where hundreds of years earlier blacks suffered through slavery, racism, and not that far back, blatant racial discrimination in virtually every segment of society and part of the country — some of which continues to this day.

Black Americans particularly had high hopes that many of their concerns and issues would be addressed — inferior schools, high unemployment, especially among black youth, violent crime, and gang-terrorized inner cities to name just a few. Black parents could tell their black children, especially boys, "See what you can become."

White Americans felt and hoped that his election signaled a new "post-racial" America. For many whites, especially many in the media, his election gave them a "thrill up the leg" showing that they and the country were not racist. He would bring America, black and white, rich and poor, together.

Both were duped.

Four years into his presidency, he answered those who felt he could do more for black America, saying in a Black Enterprise magazine interview, that, "I am not the President of Black America; I am the President of the United States of America."

However, he has not hesitated to be president of: gay rights and same-sex marriage America; extreme environmentalists and climate change America; open borders America; and protect the "dreamers" — children born to illegal immigrants — America.

As fellow Newsmax Insider Deroy Murdock wrote in March in National Review:

"Based on the Obama administration's own latest-available statistics by the most basic economic-performance metrics — with one key exception — black Americans are worse off now than when Obama was sworn in on January 20, 2009."

Murdock quoted, as have I, liberal media commentator Tavis Smiley who has said that "Sadly — and it pains me to say this — under the last decade, black folk, in the era of Obama, have lost ground in every major category."

Blacks apparently share the view that Obama has not done enough for the black community. An August Gallup poll found that a majority of blacks, 52 percent, believed that Obama had not gone far enough to help them — up from 20 percent during the 2008 campaign and 32 percent his first year in office.

They are not alone!

He also ignored the growth of ISIS, the genocide in Aleppo, Chinese expansion in the South China Sea, the Cuban people and dissidents by cozying up to the Castro's, the people of Israel, and the plight of our veterans.

As he departs, keep in mind that Obama is loved and revered by white and black liberals — and the mainstream media — not because he is black, but because he is a "black liberal."

They share no such love or affection for black conservatives who dare to have different viewpoints on solutions to many of the problems confronting black America. In fact, they have disdain for them — just ask South Carolina Republican Senator Tim Scott or Supreme Court Justice Clarence Thomas.

Obama is a great role model as a loving and caring husband and father. And, his "My Brother's Keeper" mentoring effort is commendable. However, he, the black president, could have done so much more from his bully pulpit to bring attention to the importance of family related problems facing much of America's black communities.

He could and should have addressed the problem of the over 70 percent black illegitimacy rate and the consequences of having children out of wedlock; tell youth to stay in and do well in school; respect parents, teachers and those in authority and, urge young black men to take care of and help raise their children. But that was not his soapbox.

Remember, he said he was not "president of black America."

As to a "post racial" America — forget about it!

He used his Attorney General Eric Holder and their race bating allies to play the race card at every opportunity. Question his motives and you were either a racist or, if black, an Uncle Tom.

When it suited his purposes, he used race to show blacks that he "felt their pain."

Comments such as Trayvon Martin could have been his son; or, he knows what it is like to be followed in stores or have women grab their purses when he got on the elevator showed that he empathized with blacks and solidified any wavering support due to his failure to do little else for that community.

So, looking back on Obama's eight years, black and white voters have one thing in common — they were both bamboozled!

CHAPTER 3
RACE BAITING AND DIVISION

McKee: Obama's Race-Card Strategy Is Disingenuous
Wednesday, June 27, 2012 03:10 PM

In 2006, then Sen. Barack Obama went to Maryland's oldest historically black university, Bowie State, to campaign for a white Democrat who was running against black Republican Lt. Gov. Michael Steel for the U.S Senate. He said: "You don't vote for somebody because of what they look like. You vote for somebody because of what they stand for."

Two years later in 2008, black and white liberals hailed Obama's election as the dawn of a "post-racial" America — no more double standards on "race-card" politics.

What is the reality today?

Edward Klein writes in "The Amateur" that Obama's chief strategist, David Axelrod, has nicknamed him "Black Jesus;" syndicated radio show host Tom Joyner urges blacks to support Obama ". . . because he's a black man;" Chicago Bears head coach Lovie Smith says in an Obama campaign commercial: ". . . it's left up to us, as African Americans, to show that we have his back . . ."; the executive director of the Congressional Black Caucus (CBC) says that criticism of Obama is "because he's black;" The Leadership Conference on Civil rights (LCCR) tells House Speaker Boehner that Attorney General Holder should not be held in contempt of Congress because he is doing an "exemplary job" in enforcing "civil rights laws;" and, the CBC invites the IRS and ACLU to a meeting of black ministers to show them how to get around IRS rules in order to repeat Obama's 95 percent black turnout.

If Rush Limbaugh or Sean Hannity said we should elect Mitt Romney "because he's a white man;" if a white NFL head coach appeared in a Romney commercial saying: ". . . it's up to us as white Americans" to cover his back . . ." there would be an uproar with demands for sponsor boycotts and calls for NFL condemnation.

Regarding Holder, Rev. Al Sharpton quickly dealt the race card: Holder was ". . . mishandled just like the young Black and Latino men . . . who are demonized on our streets every day."

On the ministers' meeting, CBC Chairman Emanuel Cleaver, D-Mo., said it was called to discuss ". . . Jim Crow-style 'poll tax'" voter ID laws which are designed to suppress black turnout. Imagine what would happen if Ralph Reed of the Faith and Freedom Foundation had hosted a meeting featuring a George W. Bush Attorney General and the IRS telling white evangelicals how to get around IRS rules to get out their voters.

How do we go from "don't vote for somebody because of what they look like," to an almost race neutral campaign in 2008, to today when Obama's color is on the front burner — for blacks?

The Obama team knew they had the black vote "in the bag." The problem was keeping the Sharpton's and other black leftists in the closet so as not to frighten whites. Put "Oprah" out front to reassure and get enough white votes to win.

Today, she has been thrown under the bus and is nowhere to be seen. Has anyone asked her why? Many of those whites who supported Obama are having "buyer's remorse" over his failed economic and left-wing policies. So, they must repeat the 95 percent black turnout.

How? Take a page out of the old Southern Democrat racist playbook — but direct the blatant racial appeals to blacks. Bet that black voters care more about Obama's color than the color of their money; that unlike most voter groups, will not ask "what have you done for me lately?"

Frederick Harris wrote in The Washington Post that, during a Howard University speech in 2007, Obama promised to ". . . ensure fairness in the criminal justice system; assist in passing a federal racial-profiling law; encourage states to reform their death penalty laws . . . and rethink the wisdom of locking up first-time nonviolent drug offenders for decades."

They are still waiting.

What has "Black Jesus" done to pay off non-black disciples? For wealthy white elites, hobnobbing at lavish fundraisers; for Hispanics, a constitutionally dubious work permit program; for gays, repeal of "Don't Ask, Don't Tell" and non-enforcement of the Defense of Marriage Act; and for Planned Parenthood and feminists, opposition to a ban on race and gender-based abortions.

The payoff to his and the Democrats' most loyal followers suffering under 40 percent youth unemployment: avoiding black neighborhoods on his Midwest bus tour; telling blacks to stop complaining, crying, and grumbling; and, directing his surrogates to tell blacks to vote for him ". . . because he's a black man." Their response: lay palms at his feet and sing the race card hymn.

The race-card strategy is disingenuous, hypocritical and demeaning! The real reasons they do it is because he — and Holder — are black liberal Democrats!

If race were the real issue, the "defenders of blackness" would have condemned racist characterizations and comments — by black and white Democrats — against Condoleezza Rice, Colin Powell, Michael Steele, Herman Caine Congressman Allen West, R-Fla., and Florida Lt. Gov. Jennifer Carroll — black Republicans all.

Instead, they either joined the lynch party or smiled as they looked up at the tree.

Will Republicans fight back and call the race-card hand? Don't bet on it. They will probably fold so that they will not be called — you guessed it — "racists."

Obama Seen By Defenders as Black, Liberal, and a Democrat

Monday, August 13, 2012 04:35 PM

Guess what? I agree with Al Sharpton on something!

He is defending President Obama's statement that he is "not the president of black America" but is "the president of the United States of America."

Sharpton has slammed Obama's critics for holding him to a higher standard than they did for Bill Clinton. He is not alone.

Writing for MSNBC's "the Grio," Zerlina Maxwell said:

"The idea that the nation's first black president is not the representative of all black people should not surprise anyone. The president and his administration have consistently argued that "a rising tide lifts all boats . . ."

And then there is Hazel Dukes, president of the NAACP New York State Conference who said:" I think he is the president of the United States and I believe he is addressing the people regardless of race, creed or color by saying he wants to be president of all of us . . ."

Wow! Where were these folks and their allies when Jack Kemp and Ronald Reagan were criticized for using the "rising tide" analogy?

Obama's black critics have not doubted that he is the president of all Americans. Their argument is that he has not paid enough attention to the unique problems facing black America. As usual, there is no tolerance of those who would criticize him or his policies. Why? You guessed it — because he is blaaaack!

As Dr. Boyce Watkins of Syracuse University writes:

"Nearly every representative from [Sharpton's organization] and the NAACP marches to the beat of the same drummer when it comes to expressing unconditional, unquestionable loyalty to the Obama Administration. There is no room for constructive criticism . . . true advocacy . . . even the slightest disagreement . . . The truth is that there isn't a single thing that President Obama could say that would not meet with complete agreement from two of our leading civil rights organizations. This implies, unfortunately, that these groups work for President Obama . . . the sad fact is that we have to wonder if they care more about the Obama White House than they care about black people themselves."

As I have often said, Obama's loyalists are very disingenuous. They are not defending him because he is black. They are defending him because he is black, liberal, and a Democrat.

If blackness were the issue, they would have been supportive of Colin Powell and Condoleezza Rice when they were the first black National Security Advisers and Secretaries of State (Republican appointees of course) or of black Republicans who have run for state-wide office. To them, Obama and Democrat presidents are presidents of all of the people and get a pass.

All they have to do is go to a few black churches and say "I love ya all" and "can I get an amen?"

Sharpton and other Obama defenders are correct that he is president of all Americans. However, they miss the boat when it comes to black issues. History tells us that being president of all Americans does not mean that you cannot address problems impacting black Americans.

President Johnson was president of all Americans — and historically a staunch segregationist who fought civil rights bills — yet he — with the help of Republicans — pushed through the 1964 Civil Rights and later Voting Rights acts to help blacks.

Richard Nixon was president of all Americans, yet he initiated the concept of "Black Capitalism" to assist black businesses.

George W. Bush was president of all Americans, yet he fought to eliminate the "soft bigotry of low expectations" in order to improve educational standards and narrow the achievement gap of black students.

So what does this mean? Just because Obama is president of all Americans does not mean that he cannot have a meaningful agenda to address crucial problems impacting black America which gave him 95 percent of their vote. His black critic's stress that blacks are getting little, if any, return for their investment and are being taken for granted.

Not so for his response to his other constituencies. As president of all Americans, he had the will to: support same sex marriage; oppose legislation banning race and sex-based abortion; give a half billion dollar "Green Energy" boondoggle to Solyndra; and, spare deportation to 800,000 illegal immigrants who came to the country as children.

If he could do that for these interest groups, they ask why hasn't he addressed some of the crucial issues facing black America: gang violence, black on black crime and the slaughter of thousands, including children, in our major cities (including his own Chicago); disproportionate sentencing and incarceration rates of black males; and, atrocious unemployment rates, especially for black youth to name a few.

So, although I agree with Sharpton and others that Obama is president of all Americans, for them to give him a pass and say he has no special obligation to address key issues impacting blacks as he has others, is a huge cop out. If he were not a black liberal Democrat firmly in the pockets of the left-wing Democrat establishment, they would be all over him.

Obama Rediscovers his Race

Monday, July 22, 2013 08:44 PM

"Trayvon Martin could have been me 35 years ago."

This was the headline-grabbing quote from President Obama last week when he spoke on race and the Zimmerman verdict as he tried to explain black America's reaction to white America.

His subtle message, especially to blacks, was that: I too am black with shared experiences and I understand and feel your pain.

He went a long way toward getting his Black Mojo back and showing his black critics that he cares about and feels the pain of black Americans on the issues surrounding Trayvon Martin's shooting death.

He discussed racial profiling and his own experiences as a black man. He hit all the right racial notes:

- Racial disparities in our criminal laws.

- Disproportionate involvement of black youth in the criminal justice system.

- Trayvon Martin was statistically more likely to be shot by a peer.

- The need to spend time thinking about how to bolster and reinforce young black boys who are getting a lot of negative reinforcement.

- Bringing business leaders, clergy, celebrities, and others together to determine how to do a better job helping young black men feel that they have pathways and avenues to succeed.

Where has he been?

He has had five years to discuss these and other issues facing blacks: higher incarceration and sentencing rates, double-digit unemployment and black-on-black crime to name a few but has avoided anything dealing with an "urban" agenda.

Millions for Obamacare but no agenda to attack these problems.

Why?

He told us in May ". . . the middle class will always be my number one focus. Period."

And what about the poor and the problems facing blacks that he so eloquently voiced in his remarks?

A new study by Georgetown University's Center for Applied Research shows that Obama ranks dead last with his oval office predecessors in making references to the "poor" — only 26 percent!

This compares to George W. Bush's 67 percent, Bill Clinton's 61 percent and Ronald Reagan's 65 percent.

Will he change this pattern in his upcoming speeches on the economy?

Probably not.

That's one reason he has been accused of avoiding black issues.

Writing in this space in February I quoted noteworthy blacks who were "speaking out against the president's benign neglect" of black people:

- Former U.N. Ambassador Andrew Young who told Newsmax TV that criticisms of Obama for not dealing with issues facing black Americans were "warranted and necessary."

- Miami Herald columnist Leonard Pitts Jr. who wrote that Obama had "assiduously ignored" race and described him as being "mute" on the subject . . ."

More recently, Tampa Bay Times columnist Bill Maxwell wrote:

"Well into Obama's second term . . . many who worked tirelessly and donated money to get the then-Illinois senator elected are quietly voicing their disappointment. A rare few are publicly acknowledging the growing perception that Obama lacks genuine interest in their issues."

Perhaps Obama's "I feel your pain" remarks will let him off the hook as far as doing anything regarding black issues. All is forgiven — even his ""shake it off. Stop complainin" message to the Congressional Black Caucus.

As to "entertainers," who is he referring to?

His good friend, text buddy, White House guest and foul mouth rapper Jay-Z who is notorious for lyrics filled with the "N" word and other disgusting language?

If so, will he tell Jay-Z and other black rappers to knock off the gutter stereotypical minstrel show caricatures of black men and references to "hoe's", "glocks on the hip and "N-----s?"

Will he tell his friends and donors in the entertainment industry that much of their music and images add to the "negative reinforcement" he mentioned in his remarks?

Fox Sports columnist Jason Whitlock recently wrote:

"Thug rappers and their employers are partially to blame for Zimmerman seeing a black kid in a hoodie and immediately thinking 'punk criminal.' The same group is also partially responsible for making young people think its cooler to pose as a wannabe thug than a wannabe scholar . . . the rap industry, the record labels and the commercial artists preach a message to young black people expressing "the most unethical, intimidating, violent, divisive and classless behavior . . ."

Don't expect the Revs. Sharpton and Jackson, NAACP, Congressional Black Caucus, or Attorney General Eric Holder to speak out against the entertainment industry's glorification of the thug image of black youth that often leads to racial profiling or black-on-black crime.

Marches in 100 cities against black-on-black crime, gang violence or protests outside major entertainment companies objecting to Jay-Z type lyrics?

Don't bet on it.

Will they heed the advice of Tampa City Councilman Frank Reddick?

". . . No one is speaking about black-on-black crime, and that's the problem in our community . . . We need to make some changes, and I hope we start soon."

Regarding any effort to repeal Stand Your Ground laws in the states that have adopted them, marchers, Obama, and Holder are all wasting their time.

Republicans outnumber Democrats in state legislatures and control both chambers and the governors' offices in 23 states. Black legislators, who are mostly Democrats, really have no power in those states to change anything without GOP support.

In Florida, for example, the GOP has the governor's office, a 26-14 majority in the Senate and a 76-44 majority in the House.

Good luck!

Support for Police Is Too Little Too Late

Tuesday, December 23, 2014 10:45 AM

Barack Obama, Eric Holder, Mayor Bill de Blasio and the Rev. Al Sharpton did not pull the trigger that killed two New York police officers.

Neither did the "Hands Up-Don't Shoot" false narrative gestures of athletes and members of the Congressional Black Caucus and the "racist police" video of actor Samuel L. Jackson.

But there should be no doubt that their collective inflammatory anti-cop rhetoric and actions helped create the atmosphere for the ambush assassination of police officers Wenjian Liu and Rafael Ramos.

They were joined by countless others in uncontrolled and often violent protests and more incendiary rhetoric.

More recently, we witnessed "Occupy Wall Street" type protesters throughout the nation freely rampaging through department stores, blocking streets and bridges, and challenging police. In New York, Mayor de Blasio sided with protesters and bashed the media. His response to attacks on his own police was that they were "alleged" and was silent when they chanted: "What do we want? Dead cops. When do we want it? Now."

This tragedy shows very vividly that playing racial politics can be deadly when a confused and cowardly mind like Ismaaiyl Brinsley decides to act upon their hateful rhetoric.

It should be noted that when protesters want dead cops, they include all cops — black, white, Asian, and Hispanic. They disrespect the badge and the uniform regardless of the race or ethnicity of the person wearing it. Just look at the cops Brinsley slaughtered — a Hispanic and an Asian. He didn't care what they were — they were cops!

Now, some of the main practitioners of racial divisiveness and blanket anti-cop rhetoric are among the first to express sorrow and urge peace and support for the police.

The Rev. Al Sharpton: "We do not believe that all police are bad, nor do we believe that most police are bad. We must unite and work to heal our city and this nation."

Attorney General Eric Holder: "These courageous men and women routinely incur tremendous personal risks, and place their lives on the line each and every day, in order to preserve public safety. We are forever in their debt."

President Obama: "The officers who serve and protect our communities . . . deserve our respect and gratitude . . . I ask people to reject violence and words that harm, and turn to words that heal — prayer, patient dialogue, and sympathy for the friends and family of the fallen."

And then there is de Blasio. What a turnaround!

After months of anti-cop rhetoric including saying that the Garner case "is not based on decades of racism, this is based on centuries of racism," he sang a different tune at a press conference.

After giving implicit consent to the conduct of the protesters, he now wants to find some way to move forward "away from anger and hatred" and "bring police and community together." He even said that there can be no violence against "those who protect us" and that he has "respect for the police."Eloquent comments all — but too little too late.

The president, Holder, Sharpton, and de Blasio showing respect and gratitude for the police — after these tragic murders — is a bit disingenuous.

Did it take the murders for them to realize that all cops aren't bad and we should show gratitude for their service? Where have they been?

Although they could have combined criticism and concerns over police conduct in certain instances with expressions of support and need for the police, they did not.

And, where were all of those civic, political, religious, and community leaders in New York who are now expressing such sadness over the murders of the two officers?

I do not recall any black or Hispanic elected officials, civil rights or civic leaders in New York, or elsewhere, calling press conferences condemning the hateful "dead cops" rhetoric or attacks on police prior to the assassinations and during the protests.

Where were their press conferences in support of the police who protect their communities?

So, what happens now?

Will de Blasio continue to value Sharpton's advice as his trusty race relations adviser over that of his police commissioner?

Can he govern when he has lost the respect of 35,000 New York police officers?

Will he work with and listen to black and Hispanic elected officials — or Sharpton?

As to the president: Will he take time from his sanctuary vacation retreat to come before the press, as he did in the Henry Gates, Trayvon Martin, Michael Brown, and Eric Garner cases, and show appreciation for law enforcement? And condemn inflammatory rhetoric?

Will he send three White House officials to the funerals of officers Liu and Ramos as he did to the Michael Brown funeral?

We will soon know.

Rush Was Right: So Much for 'Hope and Change'

Tuesday, January 19, 2016 04:24 PM

It's been quite a week for Barack Obama. He gave his final State of the Union message and announced the implementation of the Iranian nuclear accord.

No doubt Obama wants the Iranian deal to be considered a key part of his legacy notwithstanding that many believe he and his negotiators were hoodwinked into a sell-out plan putting Iran on a clear path to nuclear weapons and bankrolling terrorist surrogates like Hezbollah and Hamas.

The Hail Mary agreement reeks of appeasement and comes as the Obama administration enters the last minutes of its "4th quarter" hoping to put points on Obama's "legacy" scoreboard. The question is whether that score will be on the winning or losing side.

So how is the tally shaping up?

The mainstream media and Democrats went ballistic when radio show host Rush Limbaugh said in 2009 that he hoped Obama would fail.

Now that Obama's presidency is almost over, when one puts his domestic record in the rear-view mirror, Limbaugh was right to hope he would fail.

Limbaugh's concern was Obama's liberal agenda and that if he succeeded it would be bad for the country: "Liberalism is our problem . . . I know what his plans are, I don't want them to succeed . . . the absorption of as much of the private sector by the U.S. government as possible, from the banking business . . . to health care."

He asked what was so strange about wanting Obama to fail if his mission was to restructure and reform the country so "that capitalism and individual liberty are not its foundation."

Limbaugh's fears have been realized.

Obama said that his goal was to "fundamentally change the United States of America."

In many ways he and his fellow Democrats have succeeded, not failed, and the transformation is fully underway: the Affordable Care Act (Obamacare); usurping the legislative function of Congress by executive order; unblemished support for federal funding of Planned Parenthood, and pandering to abortionist and "green" lobbies; overseeing a growing entitlement nation; using the IRS to bully conservative political groups; seeking a "You didn't build that" redistribution of wealth society; and, instituting a "blame America first" foreign policy.

On the other hand, there are those who will argue that Obama has been a failure and harmed the nation not only because of the above policies, but also because of his lapses in leadership.

In foreign affairs, his "lead from behind" strategies have resulted in America having little if any credibility and respect around the world.

In the Mideast, particularly, former allies believe that the United States is no longer a reliable partner to be trusted especially after the one-sided Iran deal. He is considered a weakened president, limping his way toward the final whistle ending his eight year game trying to change the country and apologize to the world for what he considers the nation's missteps of the past.

On terrorism, while he is silent on the slaughter of Christians, he refuses to use the term "radical Islamic terrorism" as if he for some reason is afraid to offend Islamic terrorists who are unleashing death and misery all over the globe — including here at home.

Domestically, he is spending the nation into oblivion with a deficit of $18.9 trillion and rising in a seemingly limitless economic recession; picks and chooses which laws to ignore; appears to view immigration "reform" as a means to ultimately "transform" the complexion of the electorate; and, instead of improving race relations as was the nation's hope, he has polarized them to firm up his black base as needed.

What is really sad is that the first black president's greatest failure has been to black America.

As author and television host Tavis Smiley has said, "Black folk in the era of Obama have lost ground in every major economic category."

Smiley accurately points out that blacks were "caught up in the symbolism" of the Obama presidency. Unfortunately, so were most of the pandering black political, academic, and civil rights leadership.

Although he managed tears referring to the death of black youth in Chicago at his gun control press conference, during his two terms he has not lifted one finger to take action against "war zone terrorism" of black on black violence, bloodshed, and urban blight and fear in Chicago and other major cities — most of them controlled by Democrats.

As Marian Wright Edelman, founder and President of the Children's Defense Fund, recently said "there have been 16 times more boys lost to gun violence since 1968 than all of those who were ever lynched."

Yet, the president has shown more empathy for and taken more action to assist the children of illegal immigrants than he has in addressing the murder and mayhem among his own people in his own country.

It is both ironic and sad that in this week of the celebration of Dr. Martin Luther King, Jr.'s birth, the score board on the legacy of the first black President of the United States appears to be one of failure to the world, country — and black America.

Many believe that he just might wind up being regarded as one of the worst presidents in modern times. So much for "hope and change.

Obama Divides on Race

Thursday, July 14, 2016 01:56 PM

Barack Obama never misses an opportunity to play the race card and pander to a constituency — even at a memorial service.

The last thing the families, friends, and colleagues of the five assassinated Dallas police officers needed or wanted was a lecture by the president on the legacies of slavery, Jim Crow, racial discrimination, and the availability of guns.

If you want to see excellent models of fostering good race relations and healing divisions, look not to the president, but to three fantastic individuals whose light shone bright during the Dallas tragedy: Dallas Police Chief David O. Brown who unified his city; Parkland Hospital trauma surgeon Dr. Brian Williams, who expressed support for police while acknowledging his mistrust; and, shooting victim and mother Shetamia Taylor, who praised the police who shielded her and her sons from a shower of assassin's bullets.

They all showed that that it is possible to have compassion for the legitimate concerns about black men's interactions with the police ("driving while black") and yet express support and compassion for law enforcement.

Unfortunately, too many really don't want an honest discussion on race. They want to exploit raw emotions. It starts at the top.

The president and his attorney general have been quick to send the Department of Justice to investigate the killing of blacks by police and say that LGBT and Hispanic victims in Orlando were "often victimized by crimes of hate."

But it took the president five days — until their memorial service — to publicly call the slaying of the five police officers by a black assassin "a crime of racial hatred."

In the aftermath of the Louisiana and Minnesota shootings, the president and Hillary Clinton immediately resorted to pandering: Obama referred to the "legacy of slavery and Jim Crow," and Clinton rubbed salt on wounds by reciting the names of blacks killed by police.

If the victims are black as in Charleston or Hispanic or members of the LGBT community as in Orlando, the Obama administration is quick to blame hate.

But when a black man killed five white cops in Dallas, Obama initially refused to call it a hate crime saying that it was "very hard to untangle the motives of this shooter" — even after the shooter told police he wanted to kill white people and white cops.

No one can take the president seriously when he remains silent while Chicago reportedly has recorded 3,470 murders since Obama took office, 319 homicides this year — more than New York and Los Angeles combined — and over 2,000 shooting victims thus far in 2016!

An honest conversation on race would mean that the president and attorney general would be as quick to call a press conferences to condemn this bloodshed in Chicago and other urban centers as they have been police shootings of blacks.

It seems that a black life — even that of a child — is cheaper if taken by another black?

And then there is the hypocritical comment by Clinton that white people must listen to black people. She can start by telling her teachers union supporters to listen to black people and stop opposing choice and vouchers for poor black students so they can have access to the same high-quality education that her daughter and the President's have received!

But don't worry. That conversation won't take place!

Hillary won't do anything to improve the plight of blacks in our cities and relieve law enforcement of having to do so much of the "shovel work" on social problems that Chief Brown referred to — mental health, drug addiction, failed schools, single mother households — conditions which Clinton and her liberal Democrat political allies' policies have tolerated and perpetrated for decades — and most of which Obama has ignored during his presidency.

Blacks' priorities have been all but invisible to Obama. He has spent his time addressing issues impacting other constituencies, until he needed to invoke his "blackness" by appeasing the Black Lives Matter crowd by attacking law enforcement.

He even went as far as to compare that movement with the civil rights, abolitionist, woman's suffrage, and environmental movements. I do not recall those movements' marchers shouting "Pigs in a blanket fry them like bacon," throwing bricks at police or burning businesses.

All of us should listen to and heed the words of 15-year-old Cameron Sterling, son of Alton Sterling who was killed by police in Baton Rouge last week. "I want everyone to protest the right way . . . with peace, not guns, not drugs, not alcohol, not violence . . . people . . . no matter what race, should come together as one united family."

That's the right message — not the one that the president sent by refusing to light up the White House in blue in honor of the slain Dallas officers as he did to celebrate the Supreme Court same-sex marriage ruling.

CHAPTER 4

INSENSITIVITY TO BLACK ISSUES AND URBAN VIOLENCE

Blacks Lose Whether Obama — or Romney — Wins

Tuesday, November 6, 2012 12:12 AM

Clarence V. McKee's Perspective: Regardless of the victor today, black voters are in deep political trouble.

Democrats will continue to take African-Americans for granted and ignore critical issues facing people of color if President Barack Obama manages a repeat of his 2008 black voter support.

If GOP presidential nominee Mitt Romney wins, Republicans will step up efforts to attract non-Cuban-American Hispanics, youth, and women, at the expense of black voters.

GOP strategists who say outreach to blacks is a waste of time will have prevailed.

The efforts of Presidents Nixon, Reagan, Bush Sr., and Bush Jr. (not to mention Jack Kemp) to attract more blacks to the base of the party could become history.

In either case, the power of blacks as a relevant voting block at the national level could be lost for years. The focus instead will be on Hispanics — the nation's largest-growing ethnic voter group.

Black influence at the state and regional levels is just as ominous.

A July article in The New Orleans Times-Picayune sums it up: "Black political power vanishes across the South."

The newspaper quotes David A. Bositis of the Joint Center for Political Studies.

"Black voters and elected officials have less influence now than at any time since the civil rights era," according to Bositis. "Black state legislators, generally elected in black majority districts . . . are now almost entirely isolated in the minority. Republicans . . . dominate . . . statewide political offices in these states. Virtually all black elected officials in the region are outsiders looking in."

How did it come to this?

Hispanics, Asians, and women do not put all their political eggs in the Democratic Party basket as blacks do. Therefore, they — like independents — are sought after by both parties.

Why are blacks in this precarious position after centuries of struggle and bloodshed? Some blame it on plain political stupidity.

William Reed, who is black, wrote in the Florida Courier that "the course Obama is on has caused blacks' conditions to worsen over the past three years."

Citing disproportionately poor employment rates and an increased need for federal assistance such as food stamps, he said that blacks "have accepted a level of leadership the majority of Americans see as subpar."

On issues such as strengthening families, unemployment/economic empowerment, drug use, and incarceration, he said that Democrats are as "derelict as Republicans" and asked: "How dumb are we? Where are our demands for representation?"

Unlike Reed, much of the black political and civil rights establishments do not hold Obama accountable. Joined by black celebrities like Stevie Wonder and Morgan Freeman, and rappers Jay-Z and Pitbull, they are mobilizing blacks to repeat the 95-96 percent support they gave Obama in 2008.

But Oprah is nowhere to be seen!

Obama is doing his best to get crucial female, Hispanic, Jewish, white, and independent voters and has virtually ignored the black community.

He assumes his loyal shepherds will herd their black flocks into his corral, telling them to "Shake it off; Stop complaining; Stop grumbling; Stop cryin."

Is there any hope?

It won't take much of a crack in that 2008 black vote to doom Obama's chances, especially when combined with expected defections from whites and independents.

A silent minority of blacks doesn't want to be ignored and is expressing disenchantment.

One black woman and former Obama supporter lamented to an interviewer: "When is the last time he went to the 'hood' in Miami, Cleveland, or his hometown of Chicago? He caters to every group but us."

In Ohio, Kenneth Price, a lifelong Democrat and ordained minister who supported Obama in 2008, reportedly said that Obama's embracing same-sex marriage "was the last straw for me," and expressed anger over Obama's stance on abortion: "We've had 54 million babies murdered in this country."

Former Ohio Secretary of State Kenneth Blackwell, who is black, was quoted as saying that issues of marriage, life, and the high black unemployment rate "have fed discontent and provides an opportunity for swinging 6 percent."

A coalition of black pastors has launched a national campaign to rally blacks against Obama because of his same-sex marriage stance. And, the rapidly growing black pro-life movement is critical of Obama's support of abortion, including Dr. Alveda King, niece of Dr. Martin Luther King, who said "we need jobs, not abortions."

The 14 percent black unemployment rate also has shaken the faith of many blacks as reflected in the question posed to Obama at the first debate by a black undecided voter.

"Mr. President, I voted for you in 2008," the voter began. "What have you done or accomplished to earn my vote in 2012?"

So what can stop the slide to black political irrelevancy?

First, if only 5-8 percent of Obama's 2008 black voters defect and put their pocketbooks, children, and religious principles before race and party, it would cause a political earthquake. Combined with expected white, Hispanic, and independent defections, there could be a tidal wave to send the president back to Chicago.

Second, if Romney wins, he should mention "inclusion" in his acceptance speech; abandon the GOP establishment's benign neglect of black Republicans and black voters; and, listen to advisers such as Florida Lt. Governor Jennifer Carroll; Congressman Allen West, R-Fla., and campaign strategist Tara Wall on how to reach out to his black supporters and increase their numbers.

This could signal real "hope and change" and be the "fresh start" Romney mentioned in Orlando this week.

McKee: Obama's Ties to Planned Parenthood Dangerous for Black Women

Saturday, October 27, 2012 04:21 PM

President Obama cut short his Florida campaign swing because of the deadly shooting in a Colorado movie theater on the morning of July 20.

Across the country in the president's home town of Chicago, at 11:00 a.m., Tonya Reaves, a 24-year-old black woman, 16 weeks pregnant, went to a Chicago Planned Parenthood clinic to get an abortion.

Back in Florida, Obama asked for a moment of silence for the Colorado victims: "they were loved . . . they had hopes for the future and dreams that were not yet fulfilled.'

Meanwhile, back in Chicago, Tonya wasn't doing well. After bleeding for five hours — about twice as long as it took Obama to get back to Washington — Planned Parenthood finally sent her to a hospital where doctors performed another abortion procedure at 5:30 p.m.

At 10:12 p.m., Tonya went back into surgery for uncontrollable bleeding. At 11:20 p.m., probably after Obama was in bed, she was pronounced dead.

The medical examiner ruled it an accidental death and her mother has filed a wrongful death lawsuit against Planned Parenthood of Illinois and the hospital.

I am sure that the president and his soul mates at Planned Parenthood have not read the gruesome autopsy report nor told young women that this type of abortion — 16 weeks — is nothing short of heinous.

There was no asking for a moment of silence for Tonya. No reference to her being "loved . . . had hopes for the future and dreams that were not yet fulfilled . . . "

I surmise that Planned Parenthood and the abortion lobby would say that Tonya was only exercising "her right to choose" and get "adequate healthcare."

Four days after Tonya's death, on July 24 Obama was in Portland, Ore. telling crowds: "Mr. Romney wants to get rid of funding for Planned Parenthood. I think that is a bad idea"

The pro-life community is outraged over Tonya's death.

Mark Crutcher, President of Life Dynamics has asked the Cook County, Ill. State's Attorney to launch an investigation into Tonya's death to determine if criminal charges are warranted. If shown to be a homicide, he said ". . . those responsible should be on the evening news wearing handcuffs and leg irons."

Day Gardner, president of the National Black Pro-Life Union said the case was ". . . another senseless death as a black woman dies at the hand of a Planned Parenthood abortionist" and the National Black Pro-Life Coalition is demanding a criminal investigation.

So what does this have to do with Obama? He and Planned Parenthood are joined at the hip. The organization's president, Cecile Richards, is campaigning for the president, attacking Romney for wanting to end the groups' funding and for "threatening . . . to take us back . . . more than 40 years . . . and doing "everything he can to overturn Roe v. Wade.

What has happened to black babies in those 40 years since Roe v. Wade?

Black pro-life groups point out that during that time over 17 million black babies have been killed by abortions and the abortion rate for black women is almost five times that for white women.

Alveda King, niece of Dr. Martin Luther, has said that "Every three days, more African-Americans are killed by abortion than have been killed by the Ku Klux Klan in its entire history . . . we need jobs, not abortions."

Tony Perkins, president of the Family Research Council attributes these racial disparities to Planned Parenthood which he said "has preyed on minorities since its founder advocated negative eugenics . . . "

How does all of this relate to Tonya?

One month to the day after Tonya's death, Adam Cassandra writing in The Daily Caller compared Obama ads supporting Planned Parenthood to his ads implying Romney is responsible for a woman's death after Bain Capital closed her husband's steel plant.

He asked: "Considering his support for Planned Parenthood, why isn't Obama being held responsible for the death of Tonya Reaves?"

So what can be done to check the Obama-Planned Parenthood agenda?

Arizona and six other states have prohibited state tax funds from being used for abortions. In Florida, voters have the opportunity to adopt a constitutional amendment — Amendment 6 — to ban state tax funds for abortions, with certain exceptions, and restore parental consent for an abortion for a minor child.

Planned Parenthood and its allies are spending nearly $2 million to defeat it.

Romney's position on abortion, the efforts of the above seven states and Amendment 6 in Florida will save black babies' lives so that they can be "loved," have "hopes for the future," and "dreams that were not yet fulfilled …" — Obama and Planned Parenthoods' agenda might do just the opposite.

Funerals Show Obama Insensitivity and Hypocrisy

Friday, August 29, 2014 02:21 PM

Three funerals this month — of Maj. Gen. Harold Greene, Chicago student Shaquise Buckner, and Michael Brown in Ferguson, Mo., tell us much about the Obama Administration's attitudes toward the military and hypocrisy on issues of race.

Maj. Gen. Harold Greene, the two star general assassinated in Afghanistan was the highest-ranking U.S. military officer killed in combat since the Vietnam War.

One would think that the major general's funeral would have merited attendance by the president or at least the vice president.

Did the president attend or in his absence send his vice president?

No. He was relaxing in Martha's Vineyard.

He sent Defense Secretary Chuck Hagel and Army Chief of Staff Gen. Ray Odierno.

The absence of the Commander-in-Chief or his Vice President was an insult and slap in the face to our military.

Shaquise Buckner, 16 years old, was killed in a drive by shooting in Chicago, the same day Michael Brown was killed by a white police officer in Ferguson, Missouri. Yet, her death and funeral did not merit the attention by President Obama, Attorney General Eric Holder, the national news media, or civil rights leaders — as was the case with Brown's death.

No one rioted in Chicago because Shaquise Buckner was killed.

Her mother said that her daughter was a "happy teen with a sharp focus on her future," who wanted to go into forensics. "She's been on the honor roll since she's been in high school every semester. She was supposed to start school on the 19th."

Al Sharpton and Jessie Jackson, who live in Chicago, did not rush to protest her murder; the New Black Panthers did not have rallies to condemn her murder by another black; and, news networks did not rush to cover her death — or the hundreds of other black on black murders in that city.

It was different in Ferguson.

Obama's political gurus did not miss a politically correct opportunity to score points with a key political constituency by not only sending the attorney general to Ferguson, but also sending four White House aides to Brown's funeral.

Why did Michael Brown's death merit such five-star political treatment while the murder of a promising young black teen, and hundreds of others in Chicago, merited nary a comment from those rushing to judgment in Ferguson?

As I have written on numerous occasions, it is obvious from recent events that a black life is more valuable if taken by a white cop, than if by another black. If you're black and want any justice or attention paid to your being killed in a shooting, just make sure you are killed by a white person — hopefully a cop — and not another black.

Did the President send Holder to Chicago to meet with FBI agents and Justice Department Officials to probe the hundreds of blacks killed by other blacks?

Did he ask Holder to launch a major federal, state and local strike force to attack against gang and drug violence in black neighborhoods of Chicago and other urban areas?

Of course not. Why? It is only blacks killing blacks — so what?

If black leaders, politicians and civil rights groups, and the black president and attorney general don't seem to be concerned, why should whites?

You can bet your next paycheck that if blacks were killing whites in downtown Chicago in drive-by killings that the president, attorney general, governor of Illinois and mayor of Chicago would be declaring curfews, blockading streets and asking for identification.

It would not be tolerated.

But, in August of 2014, as in years before, it is not politically correct to attack black on black slaughter and gang terrorism in our big cities where law abiding blacks cower in fear on a daily basis.

There also was no apparent politically correct gain to be had by the President or Vice President in showing respect by attending Maj. Gen. Harold Greene's funeral or sending White House aides to Shaquise Buckner's funeral.

A very sad commentary.

Obama Ignores Plight of Blacks

Friday, November 28, 2014 10:47 AM

It is amazing how the president of the United States and his team only want to discuss race or issues impacting the nation's black communities when forced to do so because of some racial incident.

First there was the case of Harvard University Professor Henry Gates who was arrested in Cambridge, Massachusetts in 2009 for breaking and entering his own home.

When asked about the incident, Obama responded that the Cambridge police "acted stupidly" and that "there is a long history in this country of African-Americans and Latinos being stopped by law enforcement disproportionately."

Regarding the shooting of Trayvon Martin by white neighborhood watchman George Zimmerman, Obama said that "if I had a son, he'd look like Trayvon."

A year later, responding to the not guilty verdict in Zimmerman's trial, he said Trayvon Martin "could have been me thirty-five years ago" and went on to identify with the experiences of many black men such as being followed in stores.

And in August, there was the shooting of 18 year old Michael Brown by a white police officer in Ferguson, Mo.

Once again, Obama put on his racial sensitivity hat saying that ,while the grand jury verdict must be accepted, the situation in Ferguson "speaks to broader challenges that we face as a nation."

In Chicago the day after the verdict for a speech on immigration, he said that "if any part of the American community doesn't feel welcomed or treated fairly, that's something that puts all of us at risk and we all have to be concerned about it."

Of course, there was no mention of his hometown's tragic record of 331 black-on-black homicides between January and October of this year with nearly half of them between the ages of 17 and 25!

So, what does he intend to do about those feelings of unfairness?

Will he be submitting a major legislative initiative to on jobs, reform of the juvenile and criminal justice system, mandatory minimum sentencing and other issues impacting young black and Hispanic males including programs to crack down on gang violence?

Will he, as was suggested in this space in August "convene a White House Summit on the problems and issues related to law enforcement and minority youth to . . . find ways to dissolve the tensions between predominantly white law enforcement and black communities?"

No. He is offering a few photo-op Band-Aids.

He has asked Attorney General Eric Holder to identify "specific steps we can take together to sup a series of regional meetings focused on building trust in our communities."

He wants to bring together state and local officials, law enforcement, community and other leaders to identify steps that can be taken to make sure that law enforcement is "fair and is being applied equally to every person in this country."

Sounds nice, Mr. President, but not all of the problems impacting black Americans are caused by unequal and unfair enforcement of the law.

The problem is that Obama has had six years to develop an urban agenda to deal with these and other issues.

He can't blame Republicans because for his first two years his Democrats were in control — he just never asked! I am not naively suggesting that the president can heal the racial divide and mistrust in the country.

However, it should not take six years to try to address the underlying problems and then only do so when prompted by some race tainted event.

Obama can't take all of the blame for six years of inaction. Most black political leaders and organizations have given him a total pass. But that didn't stop some of them from throwing gasoline on the already red hot cinders of inflammatory rhetoric after the verdict.

For example, Congressional Black Caucus Chair Rep. Marcia Fudge, D-Ohio, said the decision seemed "to underscore an unwritten rule that Black lives hold no value; that you may kill black men in this country without consequences or repercussions."

How about "blacks" killed by other "blacks" Madame Chair? Do their lives mean nothing unless taken by a white?

The failure of Fudge and other national black leaders to condemn the looting and arson as strongly as they did the verdict arguably makes them apologists for the looters and arsonists.

Where were Fudge and the Revs. Sharpton and Jackson while businesses were being looted and buildings burned to the ground?

Not in Ferguson!

Will any of them replace the income of those who lost their jobs at the burned down businesses?

No!

Will any of those protesting in cities around the country go to Ferguson and help rebuild?

No!

Hypocrisy reigns.

Finally, will the Holder Justice's Department's on-going investigation ask probing questions?

- Why the announcement of the grand jury verdict was at 8 p.m. giving those who wanted to loot and burn the cover of darkness to do so which they did?

- Why, with three months to prepare for the worst after having seen the looters "playbook in August, were state and local authorities so ill prepared to deal with the repetition of violence?

- Why, after a declaration of a state of emergency days in advance and dispatching the National Guard by the Democratic governor, there were no Guard troops to protect the two dozen businesses that were burned to the ground?

- Why, if true, did the same governor not respond to pleas of the Ferguson mayor to send in the Guard in the midst of the mayhem?

Before the president's racial strategists send him to Ferguson for another "mea culpa" on race where his own Democrat leaders' incompetence and lack of preparation led to massive violence and destruction, these questions should be answered.

Hold Obama, Democrats Accountable for Blacks Disrespect
Tuesday, December 22, 2015 11:16 AM

President Obama and much of the black political and civil rights leadership have become pretty adept at expressing selective sorrow, outrage, and expressing condolences to victims of gun violence.

But it all depends on who pulls the trigger.

Last week in a tweet, Obama called a 15-year-old black football player shot to death in Knoxville, Tenn., shielding three girls from gunshots a "hero."

In an obvious reference to gun control, he asked: "What's our excuse for not acting?"

He sent representatives to the funerals of Michael Brown in Ferguson and Freddie Gray in Baltimore — both killed by white police.

And, last month in a Facebook post, he said he was "deeply disturbed" by a police video showing a white Chicago police officer shooting and killing a black teenager.

The above expressions could be considered commendable. But, given the nature of the violence and shooting gallery atmosphere in many of our cities, the concern is a bit selective.

As I have often written in this space, neither Obama nor most black civil rights and political leaders express the same feelings over the black against black genocide occurring daily in our major cities.

Blacks in Chicago are to be commended for taking their protests over the latest police shooting and alleged cover-up to the white business district instead of, as in Ferguson and Baltimore, looting and burning their own communities.

There were no such protests urging the mayor and president to take action to stop the thousands of black on black gang killings that make many Chicago black neighborhoods killing fields; and, no demands for the resignations of key city officials for the lack of city response to the litany of black on black murders.

A good example is Reverend Jesse Jackson. In one interview he complained about Chicago's 25 percent overall and 50 percent youth black and brown unemployment rates, the closing of grocery stores, drug stores, and 50 schools.

Not much said about the killings. His remedy: a "White House policy on violence and urban reconstruction."

In a similar vein, in a recent Time magazine article referring to gun violence in black communities as a "massive problem," six-time NBA champion, league Most Valuable Player, and author, Kareem Abdul-Jabaar asks, "Where's the outrage? The demand for substantive action? The address from the Oval Office?"

He went on to say, "An announcement from the Oval Office that we're intensifying our attacks on poverty to save lives, strengthen the economy and give hope to other Americans who need it now would be welcomed."

He makes good points but he should not hold his breath. The question is: why has he, Jackson, the NAACP and so many others prominent in black advocacy, including the Congressional Black Caucus, been so reluctant to demand action by the first black president to address the issues of urban violence and black on black crime?

It is really embarrassing.

So what has Obama done on the issue of urban violence and the problems plaguing black America? Not much.

Six years into his presidency — six years — he announced two initiatives: a Task Force on 21st Century Policing in response to events in Ferguson, and other cities with the goal of instituting new steps to strengthen the relationships between local police and the communities; and, the My Brother's Keeper Imitative to help break down barriers, "clear pathways to opportunity, and reverse troubling trends" for boys and young men of color.

Too little too late.No major legislative initiatives dealing with problems facing urban America even when he had a Democratic Congress. Meanwhile, he moved with "warp speed" to address issues related to same sex marriage, protecting children of illegal immigrants, and being an advocate for the abortionist lobby, and Planned Parenthood.Any "black agenda" was in the back of the first black president's priority bus. Why were urban issues not on his agenda? As he and defenders said, he was president of all America, not of black America.

The same "blinders on" attitude also applies to Hillary Clinton. She can talk all she wants to about "Black Lives Matter," racism and injustice regarding law enforcement, but, I note that she, like Bernie Sanders and Martin O'Malley, rarely, if ever, call for an outright attack on joblessness, urban poverty, and black on black violence in our major cities — all controlled by their own Democrats.

What are worse, black Democrats and civil rights leaders don't even attempt to demand answers and accountability.

That's one reason why blacks are so disrespected politically — they and their leaders engage in selective outrage. They are so quick to say that Republicans and conservatives are insensitive to the needs of blacks and urban America, while giving their Democrats, including Obama, a huge pass on poverty, unemployment, and the gamut of ills affecting urban America.

The sad truth is that they have been a day late and a dollar short when it comes to holding Obama and Democrats responsible for seven years of neglect of millions of black American families trapped in violence plagued ghettos.

———————————————————

Obama Turns His Back on Blacks, Jews

Monday, February 16, 2015 07:21 AM

In civil rights and politics, blacks and Jews have much in common. In the fight against racism and bigotry in the United States, there was no stronger bond than that between blacks and Jews.

Of those who fought against segregation in the South, other than blacks, no other group was more hated and despised by the Klu Klux Klan than Jews.

James Chaney, Andrew Goodman, and Michael Schwerner were ambushed and killed by the Klan and local law enforcement in June 1964 in Philadelphia, Mississippi.

The three young men were volunteers in "Freedom Summer" working to register black voters. Schwerner and Goodman were Jewish. Schwerner was a particular target of the local Klan and law enforcement who reportedly called him "Jew boy." On Nov. 24, 2014, President Obama posthumously awarded these civil rights martyrs the Presidential Medal of Freedom, the nation's highest civilian honor.

Politically, blacks and Jews are among the most loyal constituencies of the Democratic Party. Blacks gave Obama over 93 percent of their vote in 2008 and 2012; Jewish voters gave him 78 percent and 69 percent of their vote in 2008 and 2012 respectively.

Unfortunately, there is something else they have common: being disrespected and given short thrift by the president and his administration.

After five years in office, the president instituted the "My Brother's Keeper" initiative to address "opportunity gaps faced by boys and young men of color and ensure that all young people can reach their full potential," a commendable effort.

The problem is that thousands of black boys and young men will never reach their "full potential" because they have been or will be slaughtered in urban gang violence at rates approaching those in Afghanistan.

And, with the astronomical unemployment rates of young black men, if they avoid death in the streets, too many will wind up idle on the corner and become absentee fathers. While taking executive action and urging legislative measures to assist virtually every other constituency, the president has done nothing comparable for his most loyal constituency in six years.

While only 17 percent of black youth between 15-17 years of age live in homes with both parents and more than 72 percent of children in the black community are born out of wedlock, Obama has remained virtually silent on issues related to the survival of the black family. What an opportunity as a black father, and president, to go before major black church groups and organizations and call for a revitalization of the black family and an end to absent fathers and senseless killings!

But, as long he has Rev. Sharpton, the NAACP and the Congressional Black Caucus covering his back, he can continue to give black America the back of his hand.

Jewish Americans — and Israel — like blacks, have received similar back of the hand treatment. In fact, a December poll by the Begin-Sadat Center for Strategic Studies found that only 37 percent of Israelis believed that Obama has a positive attitude on Israel. That means that 67 percent think otherwise.

A few recent examples of Obama and his team exhibiting disrespect of Jewish sensitivities and Israel show that the 67 percent are right,

First, he initially referred to the kosher deli terrorist attack in Paris as people being "randomly" shot.

Next was his slap in the face to Jewish Americans and Jewish communities around the world in his Resolution to Congress regarding taking action against ISIS/ISIL. It singles out several ethnic groups threatened by ISIS: Iraqi Christians, Yezidis and Turkmens--nothing about Jews.

As Freshman Congressman Lee Zeldin, the only Republican Jewish member of Congress, said: "Jews should have been included."

And now we have the controversy over Israeli Prime Minister Benjamin Netanyahu's decision to address Congress to express his concerns over an agreement with Iran regarding nuclear weapons.

The President is angered by the visit because of "protocol" issues and also won't see him, so he says, because of upcoming Israeli elections; and, some Democrats are boycotting the address including two Jewish members of the U.S. Senate.

Netanyahu is firm: "I must fulfill my obligation to speak up on a matter that affects the very survival of my country."

He is right!

After all, how many of Netanyahu's critics in the United States are within a few minutes range of an Iranian nuclear warhead?

Damn few!

While blacks and Jews share commonality in the fight for civil rights and political loyalties, they also share their president's disrespect for their loyalty.

As blacks and Jews stood side by side in the fight for civil rights, they should stand side by side in rejection of the world-wide targeting of Jews and Christians by Islamic terrorists and the fight for the survival of Israel-regardless of Obama's blindness to the same.

Black Criticism of Obama

The articles in Part I have outlined in real time how Barack Obama failed black America in many key areas. What is generally not known, due to his being coddled by the major media and much of the black political, education, and media establishments, is that there have been blacks who have dared to directly and indirectly criticize his performance.

As I noted in a February 4, 2013 Newsmax article:

Some noteworthy blacks are speaking out against the president's "benign neglect" of black people:

- Congressional Black Caucus (CBC) Member Alcee L. Hastings, D-Fla., told the publishers of the nation's black newspapers that Obama consistently "disrespects the CBC, black press, and graduates of historically black colleges . . . groups . . . critical to his re-election.

- Former U.N. Ambassador Andrew Young told Newsmax TV that criticisms of Obama for not dealing with issues facing black Americans were "warranted and necessary . . ."

- Miami Herald columnist Leonard Pitts Jr. said Obama had "assiduously ignored" race and described him as being "mute" on the subject . . .

- Dr. Julianne Malveaux, economist and former president of Bennett College for Women in Greensboro, N.C. said of his 2nd Inaugural remarks: there is a reckless disregard of his strongest supporters . . . it spoke to none of us in the African-American community . . . African-Americans deserve the same focus that other communities do . . .[6]

As noted in Chapter 11, an August 2016 Gallup poll showed that 52 percent of blacks said that Obama's policies had not gone far enough in helping the black community, up from 20 percent during the 2008 campaign and his first year in office.[7]

There were blacks, however, who made note of Obama's failure to assist the black community. His response was to arrogantly strike back. He told the Congressional Black Caucus (CBC) at a 2011 dinner, when the black unemployment rate exceeded 16 percent: "Take off your bedroom slippers, put on your marching shoes. Shake it off. Stop complaining, stop grumbling, stop crying."[8] *Washington Post* columnist Courtland Milloy wrote at the time: "The unemployment rate among blacks stands at 16.7 percent… up from 11.5 percent when Obama took office. By some accounts, black people have lost more wealth since the recession began than at any time since slavery. And Obama gets to lecture us."[9]

Even Rep. Maxine Walters (D-CA) joined the Obama criticism chorus: "We're supportive of the president, but we getting tired, y'all…We want to give [Obama] every opportunity, but our people are hurting. The unemployment is unconscionable. We don't know what the strategy is."[10]

Four years later, in January 2015, seven years into the Obama presidency, incoming CBC Chairman Rep. G. K. Butterfield (D-NC) admitted things were not good in black America. He told *CQ Roll Call*: "We've been using 'conscience of the Congress' as our brand, if you will, since our founding. But we've got to do more than that because black America is in a state of emergency right now…1 in 4 black families—and 1 in 3 black children—live in poverty, while the unemployment rate for African-Americans is roughly double that for whites…We cannot continue down this path."[11]

He dared not mention Obama!

You can bet your boots that if the president had been a Republican, he would have been blamed and blistered for those conditions. The closest he came in his acceptance speech to referencing Obama was stating that "we are fighting generations of indifference on the part of those in power." One could consider that Obama, as president of the United States, was one of those *in power*.[12]

However, Crystal Wright, distinguished black writer who tweets under the name @GOPBlackChick, wasn't so generous. Writing in the *Telegraph* on August 3, 2015, in an article entitled, "Barack Obama has done zero for black people," she said that "under the leadership of America's first black president, black people have been the biggest losers" and cited several statistics listed by Butterfield.[13]

Wright was not the only black person to criticize Obama's record with black Americans. In January of 2016, prior to Obama's last State of the Union Address, PBS Host Tavis Smiley told *Fox News* host Megan Kelly that black Americans, who are Obama's most loyal supporters, "did not gain any ground" in the seven years since Obama took office. He added: "Historians are gonna have a field day trying to juxtapose how in the era of the first black president, the bottom fell out for black America. Black people were still politically marginalized, socially manipulated and economically exploited."[14]

Smiley was consistent. A year later, in a January 10, 2017, "Dear Mr. President, Hello Brother" open letter to Obama, after noting that he had voted for him twice, Smiley was blunt on his criticism: "Given that black folk have lost ground in every single leading economic indicator category over the past eight years, I'm hopeful you won't forget the debt you owe them."[15]

As noted in the Introduction, even Reverend Al Sharpton, Obama's friend, adviser, and MSNBC host, has stated that the Obama presidency was more symbolism than substance: "We're in the post-Obama generation...We have already seen a black president. We've already seen a black first family. Now, we want to know what it is going to mean. Symbolism is not enough. It's substance..."[16]

More recently, *Fox News* political analyst, Gianno Caldwell, writes of Obama at page 129 of his book, *TAKEN FOR GRANTED—HOW CONSERVATIVES CAN WIN BACK THE AMERICANS THAT LIBERALISM FAILED* (Crown Forum, 2019):

> Here was a politician who'd failed to deliver on his promises. He'd clearly prioritized the Hispanic community, the gay community, and every other Democratic voting bloc he could think of *over* the African American community who had supported him with 95 percent of their votes. More

Americans, especially black people, were on food stamps than ever before. We had a loss of homeownership, and the unemployment rate for young black men climbed as high as 48.8 percent.

That sums it up nicely.

Part I Conclusion

Part I has shown through a series of real-time articles and commentary how Barack Obama failed America's black community in a variety of areas, including illegal immigration, abortion, jobs and the economy, and general insensitivity to the problems of urban America. For that insensitivity in those areas and others of concern to black Americans, he was rewarded by not being held accountable by the black and white liberal political and civil rights establishments and the major media, including most black journalists.

Part II will focus on how President Trump's polices on illegal immigration, criminal justice reform, abortion, school choice, urban revitalization, and the economy are benefiting black Americans, while Obama's actions, or lack thereof, on those issues did not.

PART II:

HOW TRUMP IS HELPING BLACK AMERICA

CHAPTER 5

WHAT DO YOU HAVE TO LOSE?

Blacks Better Off Voting for Trump

Friday, August 26, 2016 02:54 PM

I have written often about blacks' blind loyalty to a Democratic Party plantation system that has given them little leverage in presidential politics and has been harmful to black America — especially the poor.

That's why I was so glad to see Donald Trump venture where no Republican presidential candidate has dared to venture to "tell it like it is" regarding the condition of urban black America; expose the "dirty little secrets" that no black or white Democrat will talk about; and that most black journalists and civil rights groups refuse to hold elected officials accountable for!

So, what did Trump say that is inflaming the black and white liberal Democrat establishment and their friends in the media?

He just told the truth:

- Black parents have a right to walk outside without being shot and to a good education for their children.

- Almost 4,000 have been killed in President Obama's hometown area since his presidency began.

- Our job is not to make life more comfortable for the rioter and looter.

- Our job is to make life more comfortable for the black parents who want their kids to be able to walk home safely from school and the senior citizen who wants to be safe waiting for a bus.

- There is no compassion in allowing drug dealers, gang members, and felons to prey on innocent people.

- The Democratic Party has betrayed the African-American community and its crime, education, and economic policies have produced only more crime, more broken homes, and more poverty.

And they really got upset when Trump said: "You're living in poverty, your schools are no good, you have no jobs, 58 percent of your youth is unemployed. What the hell do you have to lose?"

Every one of these statements is true! Trump's comments mirror what many black conservatives have been saying for decades.

Those criticizing Trump most likely don't live in neighborhoods within earshot of gunshots day and night and don't send their children to the inferior schools that many inner-city children are forced to attend.

So, when white Republican Donald Trump exposes the subtle classism and racism of the liberal Democrat establishment, they can huff, puff, and call him and his supporters racists all they want, but they can't deny the truth!

When was the last time we heard members of the Congressional Black Caucus who represent most of these urban terror zones, the NAACP, the National Association of Black Journalists or any black elected official in these cities raise important issues? How many black and white Democratic officials (until there are riots) have we heard calling for an end to the violence and slaughter of so many, including innocent children, in gang infested neighborhoods in Chicago, Milwaukee, Baltimore, Miami and other urban areas?

When it takes a white Republican to step up to the plate and tell the truth about the problems facing blacks in our cities, they are and should be embarrassed — all of them — black and white alike!

It's a no-win issue for Trump.

Since they can't attack him for telling the truth, they criticize him because he spoke to white audiences. If he had gone to a black audience, they would have criticized him for not daring to say it in front of a white audience because of fear of losing their votes.

It's about time a white politician went before a white audience and spoke about the issues of inner-city America! White Democrats and Republicans have historically not done that.

Trump did and for that he should be commended!

The only thing I would have added to Trump's speeches would have been to commend the great success of America's black athletes at the Olympics including Simone Biles in gymnastics; Simone Manuel, in swimming; Daryl Homer, in men's fencing; Michelle Carter in the shot put; and so many others.

This election may be black America's last chance for relevance in presidential elections for decades.

They are the only voter group that does not ask their elected officials: "What have you done for me lately." And for that, they have paid dearly!

If after Donald Trump's unprecedented direct appeal for support by a Republican Presidential candidate, 90 to 98 percent of blacks vote for Hillary Clinton, they will get what they deserve—total, yet quiet, disrespect from both Parties.

They could go down in history as being perfect political examples of the "will you respect me in the morning" syndrome and be irrelevant in Presidential politics for the next 20 years.

But, if on the other hand, 15-20 percent of a black silent majority say "we have had enough" and vote for Trump, history will be made and the Democrats' chains on black America could be cut.

CHAPTER 6
ILLEGAL IMMIGRATION AND OPEN BORDERS

Trump Reaching Blacks on Immigration
Monday, August 24, 2015 04:48 PM

It's easy to know when liberals are beginning to worry about a Republican's political message resonating with the people. If you are black, they call you an "Uncle Tom" and if white a "Racist."

And so it is with Donald Trump and his message on illegal immigration. It — and not-so subtle liberal elitist anti-south bigotry — was on full display last week in media reports on his appearance before a campaign record crowd of 30,000 in Mobile, Alabama.

MSNBC's Chris Matthews asked a reporter how many blacks were there and a Politico article referred to the appearance as "Donald Trump, Alabama and the ghost of George Wallace."

It compared Trump to segregationist Alabama Governor George Wallace — the last third party candidate to get electoral votes — because some have condemned his immigration stance as racist.

Matthews and Politico won't tell you, but many blacks have been praising Trump's message.

First was the family of black 17-year-old Jamiel Shaw Jr. who was slain by an illegal immigrant in Los Angeles. His father said on behalf of the family: "We love Mr. Trump. We're happy, because we know he spoke up and he said something."

Recently a black woman, Chanell Temple, castigated the Huntington Park, California city commission for appointing two illegal aliens as advisers. Temple said she supports Trump's immigration position "a hundred per cent" and went on to say: "My people commit a crime they go to jail. Their people commit a crime, they get amnesty."

She later told Charles Payne on Fox News, "Trump is right for bringing up this issue."

More revealing was her comment that she was fired from her job because she did not speak Spanish to which Payne responded: "you mean in your own country?"

Trump highlighting the issue strikes a chord among blacks many of whom feel, like Shaw and Temple, that they have been thrown under the immigration and amnesty political correctness bus in favor of present and potential Hispanic voters.

Thus, we have the dirty little secret that the media and Democrats have all but ignored — the undercurrent against illegal immigration and amnesty in the black community.

Talk candidly to blacks in Florida and other states with significant or growing Hispanic populations, you hear: "I was told I needed to speak Spanish if I wanted the job," "we want people who are bilingual" or "I was not promoted because I did not speak Spanish."

Of course black students should be encouraged to learn Spanish, but, for those of a different generation who don't, is it really fair for them to be punished by termination, lack of promotion, or even not being hired because they do not speak the language of a growing immigrant population?

As Louisiana Governor Bobby Jindal said during the early-bird GOP debate, "immigration without assimilation is an invasion." He later said, there is a difference between allowing people into the country who want to embrace the culture as opposed to those who want to "establish a separate culture within."

And then there is the criminal justice system which many blacks see giving preferential sanctuary city treatment to illegal aliens who commit murders, rapes and other crimes.

What cities tell blacks and illegal Hispanic citizens to "come to our city and we will protect you from the feds?"

There is a vast silent majority of black voters — Republicans, Democrats and Independent — who are angry at how illegal immigrants and their American born "anchor baby" children are America's "new protected privileged" class.

So, who speaks for them? Certainly not Hillary Clinton, Bernie Sanders, Martin O'Malley and black or white Democratic elected officials. They don't dare raise the issue of the social impact of illegal immigration on the plight of black Americans.

As A.J. Delgado wrote in National Review last month: "Democrats are chucking aside black voters in their rush to lock in the Latino vote."

Thus far, to the best of my knowledge, no candidates of either party, not even Trump, have discussed the negative impact of illegal immigration or various forms of amnesty not only on black Americans, but also on legal Hispanic immigrants and citizens.

Democrats don't dare discuss it and Republicans — as Trump is showing — have an opportunity. They would not be alone.

When Obama gave virtual amnesty to 5 million undocumented immigrants last year, leaders of Project 21, a black conservative leadership network, were very critical and quoted a U. S Civil Rights Commission finding that " illegal immigrants depress both wages and employment rates for low-skilled American citizens, a disproportionate number of whom are black men."

Will Trump focus in on this aspect of illegal immigration? Will his GOP colleagues? If so, black history is on their side.

As far back as 1853, black journalist and former slave Frederick Douglas wrote: "Every hour sees the black man elbowed out of employment by some newly arrived immigrant, whose hunger and whose color are thought to give him a better title to the place."

Dems Throw Blacks, Victims Under Illegal Immigration Bus

Friday, January 11, 2019 03:58 PM

Black support for President Trump's position on illegal immigration is growing.

Black *and* white Democrats — and the media — won't admit it, but one of the most noteworthy points the president made in his recent Oval Office speech was that "uncontrolled, illegal immigration . . . drives down jobs and wages (and that) among those hardest hits are African-Americans and Hispanic Americans."

He's absolutely right.

The major media won't tell you, but, as noted below, there are many blacks who agree!

What's so amazing about the pro-illegal immigrants posture by Democrats is the silence of most black civil rights and political leaders on the negative impact of illegal immigration — on their own communities.

It's clear that they have joined with their liberal white Democrat colleagues in assuring that the cause of illegal immigrants takes precedence over the needs and interests of black Americans — whose ancestors came to this country in chains.

That illegal immigration hurts American low and unskilled workers is not a new revelation.

Testimony before the U.S. Civil Rights Commission over a decade ago by Vernon M. Briggs Jr., of the Center for Immigration Studies — "Illegal Immigration: The Impact on Wages and Employment of Black Workers," said in part:

"Because most illegal immigrants overwhelmingly seek work in the low skilled labor market and because the black American labor force is so disproportionately concentrated in this same low wage sector, there is little doubt that there is significant overlap in competition for jobs in this sector of the labor market . . . it is obvious that the major looser in this competition are low skilled black workers."

Today, as the economy attains new heights under Trump policies in 2018, wage growth at 3.2 percent is bringing people who had stopped looking for work off the sidelines and into the job market. And with black unemployment at all-time lows, black civil rights leaders and politicians — and their white progressive counterparts — want to open the flood gates to illegal immigrants who will then compete with black and Hispanic American citizens.

Jobs are not the only issue.

Project 21, an organization of black conservative leaders, supports the president's "strong enforcement policies intended to stop the unfair strain on public services caused by illegal immigration."

Its report, "Blueprint for a Better Deal for Black America" states that programs funded through taxes are being "reduced or unavailable to black Americans in too many communities due to illegal residents taking advantage of them."

Project 21 is not the only group of black Americans supporting Trump on the issue.

My Newsmax Insider colleague, Dr. Alveda C. King, writing in her blog, "African-American Leaders Unite Around Wall to Help Avoid Looming Crisis," is joined by a half-dozen major black leaders, in "standing with President Trump in the battle for the soul of America."

Just as they do not seem to care about the impact of illegal immigration on black and Hispanic Americans, congressional Democrats (like their allies in the media) appear to have more empathy for illegal immigrants and those amongst them who kill Americans than for the victims and their families.

The nation was saddened when California police officer Cpl. Ronil Singh, a 33-year-old legal immigrant from Fiji, was shot to death Dec. 26, 2018 by an illegal immigrant and known gang member.

To the best of my knowledge, neither the two Democratic California Senators, Diane Feinstein and Kamala Harris, or U.S. House Speaker Rep. Nancy Pelosi, also a California Democrat, *called or sent condolences to his family.*

The president did.

Speaker Pelosi, Sen. Schumer and their media allies say the president was making up a crisis when he spoke of the "20,000 migrant children illegally brought into the United States" last month used as "human pawns . . . , "or the fact that women and children "are the biggest victims . . . , " or that "One in three women are sexually assaulted on the dangerous trek up through Mexico."

Whether it relates to the negative impact of illegal immigration on black employment, concern for the victims of criminal illegal immigrants, or the dangers it poses to women and children in so-called caravans, these pro-illegal immigration-anti-wall Democrats are hypocrites. For they remain silent on illegal immigrant's crimes and support and encourage sanctuary cities to protect them while many of them, as the president said, "build walls, fences, and gates around their homes."

Democrats not only want to protect illegal immigrants. They want to put them at the front of the bus to compete for benefits at state and local taxpayers' expense while they throw blacks and victims *under that bus.*

For example, Calif. Gov. Gavin Newsome, a Democrat, proposes a state funded health program to cover 138,000 young illegal immigrants. His Democratic cohort across the country, New York Mayor Bill de Blasio, is proposing a $100 million program to provide health coverage to all New Yorkers including approximately 300,000 illegal immigrants.

Speaker Pelosi and her anti-wall supporters say the wall is "immoral" — selective morality at its best!

Nothing said about the immorality of the murder of Cpl. Singh; the killing of Pierce Corcoran, the 22-year-old son of a Knoxville fire captain by an illegal immigrant; the murders of innocent children by MS-13 gang members; or, the fact that the border is a pipeline for illegal drugs that are killing Americans.

You can bet that if, God forbid, Pelosi, Schumer, Harris, Newsom, de Blasio or a hate-Trump media anchor's spouse, partner, son, daughter, or grandchild were harmed by an illegal immigrant, or suffered from a drug overdose, they would support building the wall in a millisecond!

The president should have a press conference featuring the families of victims of illegal immigrants to show the faces of grief to America to remind the nation, Democrats, and the media of *just what's at stake.*

More on Trump and Illegal Immigration

These two articles, as well as those contained in chapter 1, reiterate the point that illegal immigration hurts American lower-skilled and unskilled workers who are major losers in the competition for low-skilled jobs. Yet black and white progressives just don't seem to care. Illegal immigrants are their new favored protected class. As President Trump stated in an Oval Office address in January, as referenced above, "uncontrolled, illegal immigration...drives down jobs and wages (and that) among that hardest hit are African-Americans and Hispanic Americans."

At a time when the president's economic and related policies have brought the unemployment rate for blacks to historic lows, as was noted in chapter 11, left-wing Democrats and their presidential candidate colleagues want to open to even more illegal immigrants who will compete with blacks— and all Americans—for low-skilled and blue collar jobs. For those who won't compete in the job market, they will provide competition with legal Americans for tax dollars for public services. Not only do they want to have open borders, these "open the floodgates" apologists for illegal immigration want to protect criminal illegal aliens in sanctuary cities. Never mind having any empathy or sympathy for the victims of their crimes.

While Obama's immigration policies moved illegal immigrants to the front of his immigration bus, and Democrats' failure to act to enact legislation to correct the crises, President Trump has moved to stem the tide of illegal immigration including building the "wall" to make illegal entry, drug smuggling, and human trafficking more difficult.

As an October 2019 White House Fact Sheet points out, significant steps have been taken to stop the flow of illegal immigrants, including, but not limited to, the following:

- In September, 52,546 aliens were apprehended or deemed inadmissible at the southern border, the lowest numbers for any month in fiscal year (FY) 2019, which marked a decline of more than 60 percent from the peak in May 2019.

- September also marked the fourth consecutive month that Border Patrol apprehensions declined between ports of entry, a 20 percent decline from August. Border Patrol apprehensions have declined by an average of 26 percent each month over the past four months.

- Mexico has enhanced their border security efforts thanks to President Trump's negotiating, deploying thousands of troops to address this crisis.

- The administration has expanded the Migrant Protection Protocols to require aliens to wait in Mexico while their immigration cases proceed, reached an agreement in principle with Guatemala to have migrants apply for asylum there, and negotiated agreements with El Salvador and Honduras on asylum.

- The administration is working with other countries in the region to target human smugglers.

- The president is continuing to build the wall, with 163 miles of new border wall system under construction now and 450 miles expected to be completed by the end of next year.

- More than 977,000 aliens were apprehended or deemed inadmissible at the southern border in FY 2019—an 88 percent increase from FY 2018.

- Border Patrol apprehended more than 851,000 aliens between ports of entry in FY 2019, an increase of more than 115 percent from FY 2018. [17]

Also of note is that there is an "overwhelming number of family unit aliens and unaccompanied minors at the border" that puts an incredible strain on personnel, facilities, and local communities. For example, the Border Patrol apprehended a record 473,682 family unit aliens in FY 2019—342 percent higher than the previous record set in FY 2018 and a 52 percent increase in apprehensions of unaccompanied minors, rising to 76,000 in FY 2019.

Immigration Reform Is Not Racism

Throughout this book there have been references to how illegal immigration is most harmful to low-skilled workers, many of whom are black. Once upon a time, such workers were courted and supported by the Democrat Party as a main constituency.

Not anymore!

As stated earlier, the new favored constituency of the Progressives and Democrats are illegal immigrants, and anyone who dares challenge that favoritism and defend our immigration laws are deemed to be racists because most of those coming across the southern border are brown-skinned Hispanics.

How low can they go?

They could give a damn about the unskilled black Americans who become competitors for jobs and entry into the workforce. When all else fails, in immigration as in other areas, Democrats fall back on their old faithful standby—playing the race card!

A great example is House Majority Leader Nancy Pelosi who told a meeting of the US Conference of Mayors last year that the president's immigration plans was "a campaign to make America white again.[18]" How disgusting and patronizing to all Americans of color.

Pelosi's message was the rallying cry for Democrats to discredit the men and women of the Border Patrol, and indeed all of those who are enforcing our immigration laws, as Nazis executing a white supremacist policy targeting illegals because they are nonwhite. The most recent example of the Left's race-baiting attack on the president's immigration reform and enforcement polices is Florida Democratic Congresswoman Debbie Wasserman Shultz. At a House Committee hearing, she accused the Trump administration of pursuing a "heinous white supremacist ideology" through its immigration policies. [19]

I guess Pelosi and Wasserman Schultz don't realize that 52 percent[20] of Border Patrol agents are Hispanic!

The real story and picture of how illegal immigration has a negative impact on black low-skilled workers was pointed out by Dave Seminara in a

March 16, 2018, article in the *Los Angeles Times*, which Pelosi and Wasserman Schultz should read. He states in part:

> Claims that immigration enforcement equals racism ignore the reality that the group most likely to benefit from a tougher approach to immigration enforcement is young black men, who often compete with recent immigrants for low-skilled jobs...[21]

Seminara pointed to a Chicago example where eight hundred illegal immigrants lost their jobs in a bakery after an Immigration and Enforcement (ICE) audit forced the employer to hire new workers, "80% to 90% of whom were African Americans at higher salaries." As he stated, "in that case, and many others the beneficiaries of immigration enforcement were working-class blacks, who are often passed over for jobs by unscrupulous employers."

Do we hear any black political leaders or presidential candidates defend black workers over illegal aliens? Of course not! They are part of the problem discussed in chapter 12.

Democrats' charges of racism in Trump's immigration enforcement program are just so much hot air used to cover up their own failure to alleviate a problem that has a negative impact on their black constituents and all Americans.

CHAPTER 7
CRIMINAL JUSTICE REFORM

Black Leadership Shamefully Silent on Trump Pardons, Record Employment

Wednesday, June 13, 2018 11:10 AM

Black conservatives have often argued that the nation's black political and civil rights leadership puts loyalty to the agenda of the liberal progressive Democratic establishment above its commitment to the interests of its own people.

Judging from how that leadership has reacted to three recent events of interest to black Americans lends credence to that argument: President Trump's granting a posthumous pardon to boxer Jack Johnson; granting clemency to Alice Marie Johnson; and, historic low levels of black unemployment.

They have one thing in common — virtual silence by the black political and civil rights communities.

Jack Johnson was the first African-American world heavyweight boxing champion. His conviction and one-year imprisonment by an all-white jury in 1913 under the Mann Act for taking his white girlfriend across state lines for "immoral" purposes ended his boxing career.

Trump pardoned Johnson at the request of actor Sylvester Stallone. Over the years many others, including film maker Ken Burns and a bi-partisan group of Congressional advocates have urged multiple presidents to pardon Johnson

In 2016, then-Senator Harry Reid, D-Nev., Sen. John McCain, R-Ariz., Reps. Peter King, R- N.Y., and Congressional Black Caucus (CBC) Member Gregory Meeks, D-N.Y., petitioned Obama to grant a pardon.

The first black president did not.

Last year, Sen. Cory Booker, D-N.J., who is black, joined the group replacing retired Harry Reid saying: "…it is far past time that we honor his legacy and his life with the integrity and dignity he deserved…"

You can bet that he never thought Trump would ever do it.

After Trump pardoned Johnson, McCain praised him saying the boxing legend's "reputation was ruined by a racially charged conviction over a century ago."

Meeks deserves credit. At least he showed some class tweeting: "Jack Johnson's pardon is great news. Imagine my shock and surprise that the President and I actually agree on something."

As far as I can tell, he is the only black political figure to commend Trump.

As to Booker, who wants to be the next black president, if he made any positive comments on the pardon, after he had joined in requesting it, I have not seen them.

And where were the NAACP and the CBC?

They gave the same silent treatment to Trump's granting of clemency to Alice Johnson.

She is the 63-year-old black grandmother who was convicted and sentenced to life without parole in 1996 for her role in a cocaine trafficking operation. Ironically, Obama and his black Attorney General refused to grant her clemency in December of 2016 when he granted clemency to 231 persons including many convicted of drug related charges.

Her release was occasioned by the intervention of Kim Kardashian West who met with Trump in the Oval Office after she reached out to his Senior Adviser and son-in-law Jared Kushner.

Again, silence from black leadership.

Amazingly, the same silence from these groups came with news of the record low 5.9 per cent black unemployment rate.

Notwithstanding such historically good numbers, one is hard pressed to find, other than National Urban League President Marc Morial, any major black political or civil rights leader willing to applaud these numbers or even acknowledge the beneficial impact of the Trump economy in bringing jobs to black America.

Of course, that would not please the Democrat leadership. It's true politics over their people.

As far as I have been able to determine, only Morial has shown the integrity and honesty to acknowledge these gains — although he did hedge his bet. He said on that he was willing to "applaud the good news" and give the administration a "cup of gumbo, not a bowl…for what has occurred."

Not so with the CBC which sat on its collective Democratic hands during Trump's State of the Union Address when he mentioned the even then historically low black unemployment rate.

They have been mum ever since with some even arguing that Obama was responsible.

If Obama had overseen an economy with under 6 percent black unemployment the CBC, the mainstream media and the NAACP would be delirious.

I guess they have forgotten how he slapped them in the face in 2011 when the black unemployment rate exceeded 16 percent:

"Take off your bedroom slippers, put on your marching shoes. Shake it off. Stop complaining, stop grumbling, stop crying."

As Washington Post columnist Courtland Milloy wrote at the time: "The unemployment rate among blacks stands at 16.7 percent...up from 11.5 percent when Obama took office. By some accounts, black people have lost more wealth since the recession began than at any time since slavery. And Obama gets to lecture us."

As black newspaper publishers know, their black readers are smarter than some of their political leaders think and no doubt consider such silence a shameful betrayal of their interests.

_____

Trump, GOP Score on Prison Reform

Thursday, December 13, 2018 05:11 PM

By: Clarence V. McKee

The nation is on the verge of getting the most significant federal prison reform in decades: The First Step Act.

Thanks to President Donald Trump, Senate Majority Leader Mitch McConnel, R-Ky, and House Speaker Paul Ryan, the bill could become law before Congress adjourns.

Assuming it becomes law, let's see how many civil rights groups, black and white liberal Democrat politicians and the "hate Trump media" give Trump, McConnel, Ryan, and Senate and House Judiciary Committee Chairs Chuck Grassley, R-Iowa, and Bob Goodlatte, R-Va., respectively, any credit for getting this historic federal prison reform bill over the goal line?

The bill, among other things, would address inequities in sentencing disparities, place inmates closer to their families, allow participation in vocational training and educational coursework all designed to assist in rehabilitation and decrease recidivism rates.

As the president said, "Our whole Nation benefits if former inmates are able to reenter society as productive, law-abiding citizens."

So why is this bill needed?

Minorities, especially blacks, have long complained that the criminal justice system was two tiered — one for blacks, minorities and the poor; and, another for whites and the privileged — not unlike how the Obama Department of Justice and FBI gave special treatment to Hillary Clinton and Obama Administration operatives.

So why do we need prison reform?

According to the updated Bureau of Justice Statistics of the Department of Justice (BJS):

- About 2.5 percent of black male U.S. residents were in state or federal prison on December 31, 2016.

- Black males ages 18 to 19 were 11.8 times more likely to be imprisoned than white males of the same age.

- Black males age 65 or older were 4.4 times more likely to be imprisoned than white males age 65 or older.

- The imprisonment rate for black females was almost double that for white females.

- Among females ages 18 to 19, black females were 3.1 times more likely than white females and 2.2 times more likely than Hispanic females to be imprisoned in 2016.

- More than half (56 percent, or 6,300) of female federal prisoners were serving sentences for a drug offense, compared to 47 percent of males (75,600).

If these statistics don't raise questions about the fairness of our criminal justice system, the most recent report of the United States Sentencing Commission — "Demographic Differences In Sentencing" —should. Consistent with its previous reports, the Commission found that "sentence length continues to be associated with some demographic factors."

Among its key findings was that, "Black male offenders continued to receive longer sentences than similarly situated White male offenders."

It went on to state that, "Black male offenders received sentences on average 19.1 percent longer than similarly situated White male offenders" during the Report period fiscal years 2012-2016, "as they had for the prior four periods studied."

All is not right in our criminal justice system.

The First Step Act is a good "first step" toward penal reform.

What does all of this mean in human terms?

Utah Senator Mike Lee, a conservative Republican and major supporter of the bill put it all in perspective. He recounted in a November press release the story of Weldon Angelos, a young father of two with no criminal record who was convicted of selling three dime bags of marijuana to a paid informant over a short period of time.

What was his sentence for these nonviolent crimes in which no one was hurt? 55 years!

Because Angelos had been in possession of a gun, which was neither brandished nor discharged during the transaction, the judge was forced by federal law to give him a 55-year prison sentence.

Lee went on to state that the judge explained that the applicable federal statutes gave him no authority to impose a less-severe prison term, noting that "only Congress can fix this problem."

The First Step Act is a good beginning "fix."

To those critics of the bill who say it will cause violent criminals to be released to prey on communities, the BJS statistics contradict that argument stating that nearly half (47 percent) of federal prisoners were there for drug offenses as of September 2016 while over half (54 percent) of state prisoners were serving sentences for violent crimes at the end of 2015.

Some argue that since, as stated in the above BJS Report, only one-eighth or 12.6 percent of the 1.5 million people in prisons, are in federal prisons, that will not have a major impact.

Not true.

It is a good model for state penal reform.

States should take a close look at this bill and institute similar provisions into state laws.

For example, in Florida, which just gave ex-felons the right to vote, the new Governor DeSantis could be a hero to over a million ex-felons and their families by urging the legislature to adopt similar reforms and establish a special Commission to review prison reform in Florida's scandal ridden juvenile and adult corrections system.

As Kay Coles James, president of the conservative Heritage Foundation, said in a statement:

"The First Step Act will increase public safety, strengthen families, and give incarcerated people a chance to flourish after they've paid their debt to society. It is time to end the revolving-door our federal prisons have become and put those who are willing to work for a second chance back on the path toward reaching their full potential."

That's why the bill is called "The First Step."

More on the First Step Act and Criminal Justice Reform

Donald Trump, in his second State of the Union Address, February 2019, spoke of working closely "with members of both parties to sign the First Step Act into law" in December of 2018. As he stated, the law reformed sentencing laws that have "wrongly and disproportionately harmed the African-American community."[22]

The First Step Act gives nonviolent offenders the chance to reenter society as productive, law-abiding citizens. The president introduced Matthew Charles from Tennessee who, in 1996, at the age of thirty, was sentenced to thirty-five years for selling drugs and related offenses. The president went on to say how Charles over "over the next two decades…completed more than 30 Bible studies, became a law clerk, and mentored many of his fellow inmates." Matthew was the very first person to be released from prison under the First Step Act!

The law included measures to reduce sentences of thousands of thousands of prisoners and expand job training programs to decrease recidivism rates and relax the "three strikes rule." [23] According to the US Sentencing Commission June 2019 Report on the First Step Act, 91.3 percent of prisoners with reduced sentences were black. [24]

The president not only signed the First Step Act and mentioned it in his State of the Union Address as referenced above, but he also put the full weight of his administration behind making it work and giving a "second chance" to thousands of mostly black federal inmates. At a June 13, 2019, meeting in the East Room of the White House, attended by reality star Kim Kardashian and Cabinet secretaries, Trump announced several measures to help returning former inmates find jobs with the goal of cutting the unemployment rate formerly incarcerated people to single digits within five years. [25] Such efforts are crucial to assisting former inmates return to society and be able to live productive lives.

Former inmates have a difficult time in the job market. According to a July 2018 Report of the Prison Policy Initiative—"Out of Prison & Out of Work: Unemployment among formerly incarcerated people—formerly incarcerated people are unemployed at a rate of over 27 percent higher than the total US unemployment rate during any historical period, including the Great Depression."[26] The report also states that the rate for former black female inmates was 44 percent and 35.5 percent for their black male counterparts. For whites, the figures for white females and males were 23.2 percent and 18.2 percent, respectively.

Jack Johnson and Alice Marie Johnson

An excellent example of Obama's insensitivity to black issues and Trump's responsiveness is Trump's pardon of Jack Johnson, the first black world heavyweight boxing champion and commuting the sentence of Alice Marie Johnson, as discussed in the first article of this chapter and which is worthy of repeating, given the issues discussed in this chapter.

Jack Johnson

As stated earlier, Jack Johnson, the first African American world heavyweight boxing champion, was convicted and received a one-year prison sentence by an all-white jury in 1913 under the Mann Act for taking his white girlfriend across state lines for "immoral" purposes. It ended his boxing career.

Trump pardoned Johnson at the request of actor Sylvester Stallone. Over the years many others, including film maker Ken Burns and a bi-partisan group of congressional advocates had urged multiple presidents to pardon Johnson. Obama was petitioned in 2016 by then-Senator Harry Reid (D-NV), Sen. John McCain (R-AZ), Rep. Peter King (R-NY), and Congressional Black Caucus (CBC) member Gregory Meeks (D-NY). Sen. Cory Booker (D-NJ) replaced retired Harry Reid in 2017.

Trump pardoned Johnson—the first black president did not!

Alice Marie Johnson

As outlined in the same article, Alice Johnson is the sixty-three-year-old black grandmother who was convicted and sentenced to life without parole in 1996 for her role in a cocaine trafficking operation. Obama and his black attorney general, Eric Holder, refused to grant her clemency in December of 2016 when he granted clemency to 231 persons, including many convicted of drug-related charges. Unlike Obama, President Trump commuted Johnson's sentence. So much for Obama sensitivity!

While Obama supporters will argue that he freed record numbers of nonviolent drug offenders, he failed to make any substantial efforts on criminal justice reform until the end of his final term. [27] As to related issues of urban violence and the problems plaguing black America, especially black youth, what did Obama do?

Not much.

As noted earlier, six years into his presidency—six years—he announced two initiatives: 1) a task force on twenty-first century policing in response to events in Ferguson and other cities with the goal of instituting new steps to strengthen the relationships between local police and the communities; [28] and, 2) the My Brother's Keeper Initiative to help break down barriers, "clear pathways to opportunity, and reverse troubling trends" for boys and young men of color. [29] Worthy initiatives both. But: Too little, too late.

No major legislative initiatives dealing with problems facing urban America even when he had a Democratic Congress. Meanwhile, he moved with "warp speed" to address issues related to same-sex marriage, protecting children of illegal immigrants, and being an advocate for the abortionist lobby, and Planned Parenthood.

Unlike Trump's aforementioned efforts, any "black agenda" was at the back of the first black president's priority bus. Why were urban issues not on his agenda? As he and defenders said, he was president of all America, not of black America.

CHAPTER 8

ABORTION

Trump Says Yes to Life for the Unborn — Democrats Say No
Thursday, February 7, 2019 03:29 PM

At a time when legislation has been introduced in Congress that would make malicious acts of animal cruelty a felony punishable by fine and/or imprisonment, Democrats are silent on the issue of infanticide and late term abortions of children — *President Trump is not.*

In his State of the Union address, he said he was going to ask Congress to pass legislation to prohibit the late term abortion of children.

Why is this noteworthy?

Democrats are quietly celebrating the furor over Virginia Governor Ralph Northam's racist medical school yearbook picture because it took attention away from his earlier comments justifying infanticide.

Because of the photo, he faced almost universal condemnation and requests from Democrats for him to resign.

This is quite a contrast to the silence from the same group and most of the media to his virtual endorsement of infanticide a few days before.

During a radio interview, he said that after an "infant" deemed nonviable is delivered, it would be kept comfortable, resuscitated and "a discussion would occur between the mother and physicians."

In other words, they would determine whether the baby would be killed!

Then came the yearbook picture fiasco — Democrats were off the hook on the infanticide remarks!

For them, it appears to be easier to criticize and condemn racism than killing babies.

They also have been silent on New York State's new abortion law that allows abortion until birth, for any reason.

While Democrats have been silent on these pro-infanticide proposals and comments, President Trump has not.

In his Address, he charged lawmakers in New York with having "cheered with delight" after passing the above legislation which he described as allowing a baby to be "ripped from the mother's womb moments before birth."

He also accused Northam of "basically" saying that "he would execute a baby after birth."

If you think that's bad, just look at Vermont.

It may enact a law that would have no limitations on abortions.

As outlined by Wesley Smith in National Review the law would mean:

- "A healthy, viable baby could be killed at 8 months, thirty days gestation."

- "Abortion could be delayed or done in a manner to permit organ harvesting."

- "A fetus whose brain was sufficiently developed to experience pain could be torn slowly apart in the womb in the most agonizing manner."

- "Allow sex-selection abortion."

- "And, if it were ever possible to determine, termination to prevent a gay baby from being born."

All of this brings to mind Dr. Kermit Gosnell. He was the Philadelphia abortionist — whom I described in this space as the "black angel of Death" — who was convicted of three counts of first degree murder and sent to prison for life for stabbing infants to death after delivering them alive.

These states might welcome others like him with open arms.

Such pro-infanticide measures are not limited to states. Just this week, Senate Democrats blocked a Republican bill that would have required that babies surviving an abortion be kept alive and "immediately" sent to a hospital.

Senator Marco Rubio, R-FL., was right when he said:

"Senate Democrats, like their colleagues in Virginia and New York, seem to have no issue publicly supporting legal infanticide."

Democrats — and all people of color — should be very cautious about endorsing proposals that mirror some of the gruesome practices of the infamous Nazi Auschwitz concentration death camp physician Dr. Joseph Mengele's experiments with pregnant women and children.

The real disgrace in the abortion debate is how many black elected, political, and civil rights officials have turned a blind eye to the impact of abortion on their own people.

Like former president Obama, they have been coopted and are joined at the hip with the abortion lobby and Planned Parenthood. As I said in 2012, such ties are "dangerous to Black women."

This is illustrated by fellow Newsmax Insider, Dr. Alveda King who writes in Townhall,: "Black women are significantly more likely to undergo an abortion than are women from any other racial demographic, resulting in the deaths of an estimated 19 million black babies since Roe v. Wade."

There are other ramifications.

If Democrats supporting infanticide and late term abortion have their way, hospitals treating and caring for children with congenital deformities and conditions, such as the Shriners Hospital for Children, could have reduced caseloads in the future since such children could be terminated either in the womb or at birth.

Going into the 2020 presidential sweepstakes, Democrats have a choice:

They can, as Trump said, reaffirm the fundamental truth that "All children — born and unborn — are made in the hold image of God."

Or, they can choose the Mengele option.

Gosnell Gets More than He Gave — Life
Wednesday, May 15, 2013 05:25 PM

Dr. Kermit Gosnell, Philadelphia's "black angel of death" has given himself what he deprived his infant victims of — a chance to live!

After being found guilty of first-degree murder for the gruesome killing of three babies born alive after botched abortions, Gosnell took the coward's way out. He struck a deal to avoid the death penalty and chose "life" without parole.

This coward was also found guilty of:

- involuntary manslaughter related to an adult patient who died after a botched abortion;

- 21 out of 24 felony counts of illegal abortions beyond Pennsylvania's 24-week limit; and,

- all but 16 of 227 misdemeanor counts of violating the 24-hour informed consent law.

Planned Parenthood issued a post-verdict statement saying that ". . . we must have and enforce laws that protect access to safe and legal abortion, and we must reject misguided laws that would limit women's options and force them to seek treatment from criminals like Kermit Gosnell."

Note that the statement said nothing about the innocent babies slaughtered over many years and definitely no mention of the need for inspection and regulation of birth control clinics. The organization's concern was "access" to abortions.

We are left to assume that, from Planned Parenthood and other pro-abortion groups' perspective, laws that would "limit women's options and force them to seek treatment from criminals like Kermit Gosnell" would include inspection of such facilities on a regular basis.

Don't hold your breath for Planned Parenthood, other pro-abortion groups and their allies in the Democratic liberal establishment to seek more oversight of abortion clinics to prevent more Gosnell-like horrors. Like Senate Majority leader Harry Reid, they oppose efforts to tighten regulations on abortion clinics because they view them as threatening access to abortions. That sounds like the rationale Pennsylvania used to avoid such inspections in the case of Gosnell.

If there was any good to come out of the Gosnell trial, in addition to his conviction, it was the effort of two House Committees to gain information on how states monitor and regulate abortion clinics.

The first was directed to state Attorneys General by House Judiciary Chairman Bob Goodlatte, R-Va., and Constitutional and Civil Justice Subcommittee Chairman Trent Franks, R-Texas. It said in part:

"We have all been shocked by the tragedy in Pennsylvania . . . We are simply writing to gather information . . . to see how the federal government might partner with states to help prevent similar atrocities."

The information requested includes:

- Asking whether prosecutors treat the deliberate killing of newborns, including those newborns who were delivered alive in the process of abortions, as a criminal offense, and, if so, have there been any prosecutions?

- Asking whether state legislatures have enacted laws specifically to protect newborns delivered alive in the process of abortions?

- Asking whether abortions performed after the state's statutory limit have resulted in prosecutions.

The second initiative was led by House Energy and Commerce Committee Chairman Fred Upton, R-Mich., who sent letters to state health officials stating:

"The criminal investigation and trial of Dr. Kermit B. Gosnell of Philadelphia, Pa., raises troubling questions about the practices of abortion clinics, and whether state departments of health are aware, or even conducting appropriate monitoring, of these facilities . . ."
Among other things, the letter requested information related to:

- licensing of abortion clinics and providers

- revoked or suspended licenses of abortion clinics

- inspections of such clinics, including numbers and manner of inspections each year from 2008-2013

- procedures for monitoring and investigating complaints or adverse health events related to abortions

- disciplinary actions taken by the state against "facilities or healthcare providers" related to abortions and,

- copies of any rules or regulations governing abortion facilities or providers

Upton was joined by Committee Vice Chairman Marsha Blackburn, R-Tenn., Chairman Emeritus Joe Barton, R-Texas, Health Subcommittee Chairman Joe Pitts, R-Pa., Oversight and Investigations Chairman Tim Murphy, R-Pa., and Vice Chairman of the Oversight and Investigations and Health Subcommittees Michael C. Burgess, M.D., R-Texas. If such information is compiled it would be the abortion lobby's worst nightmare not to mention that of its Democratic allies.

How many Gosnell's are out there?

Anti-abortion groups such as Life Dynamics, Inc., Live Action and black prolife groups say Gosnell is not an aberration — he is just the tip of the iceberg!

Let's hope the horrible revelations of the Gosnell grand jury report and the grizzly testimony at his trial will lead to a re-examination of the age of viability for abortions by state legislatures — less than Pennsylvania's 24 weeks (6 months).

Planned Parenthood and congressional Democrats would probably fight the above requests. The would view any legislative re-examination of the viability period or, the monitoring of clinics as "misguided laws that would limit women's options and force them to seek treatment from criminals like Kermit Gosnell."

But, there is one thing they don't dare refute after this verdict: killing a baby born alive after a botched abortion is murder and those who participate are murderers!

So what is the difference between killing a baby just born and killing it a few seconds earlier in the womb? Some would argue none at all — murder is murder, infanticide is infanticide.

As for Gosnell, he had better start watching his own neck. Baby killers are not well regarded in prison.

More on Obama versus Trump on Abortion

As was noted earlier in chapter 4, "Obama's Ties to Planned Parenthood Dangerous for Black Women," Obama and Planned Parenthood were "joined at the hip," referring to the organization's president campaigning for him in 2012.

He was "deeply committed" to abortion rights and opposed congressional efforts to ban taxpayer funds for abortion.

I also noted that "Black pro-life groups point out that during that time (since Roe v. Wade) over 17 million black babies have been killed by abortions and the abortion rate for black women is almost five times that for white women..."

I went on to quote Dr. Alveda King, niece of Dr. Martin Luther King Jr. and director of Civil Rights for the Unborn and pastoral associate for Priests for Life. She has said, "Every three days, more African-Americans are killed by abortion than have been killed by the Ku Klux Klan in its entire history...we need jobs, not abortions."

Dr. Alveda King's Letter to President Trump on Abortion

On January 25, 2019, Dr. King wrote an open letter to President Trump, joined by leaders in the black prolife movement, thanking him for his "continuing leadership to promote human dignity and the sanctity of human life" and asking him to declare that the "abortion of a pre-born human beings is a national crisis...The scourge of abortion of human beings in the womb is an American crisis. Please declare that abortion of pre-born human beings is a national crisis." [30]

She went on to say, "One third of the babies aborted in America are African American babies while we remain the least of these in numbers of population (about 12 percent)," adding that "abortion is another form of slavery; with the human child in the womb held hostage."

She concluded, "Mr. President, we the undersigned individuals urge you to make a public declaration to this effect; that abortion of a child in the womb is a crime against humanity."

As Dr. King said in her letter, one-third of babies aborted in the country are African American while blacks are "about 12 percent." That obviously was of no concern to Obama, who catered to the proabortion lobby his entire political career.

Rich Lowry, in an August 23, 2012, POLITICO article, "Obama the Abortion Extremist" summed it up nicely.

> President Obama is an extremist on abortion. He has never supported any meaningful restriction on it, and never will.
>
> He opposed a partial-birth abortion bill in Illinois, even as the federal version passed the House with 282 votes and the Senate with 64 votes and was signed into law by President Bush in 2003. He arrived in the U.S. Senate in time to denounce the Supreme Court's ruling upholding the ban.
>
> In 2007, he told the Planned Parenthood Action Fund that his first act as president would be signing the Freedom of Choice Act. The act would enshrine in federal law a right to abortion more far-reaching than in Roe v. Wade and eliminate basically all federal and state-level restrictions on abortion. [31],

President Trump, on the other hand, is a strong supporter of the sanctity of life and anti-abortion. His recorded remarks before the 46th Annual March For Life leave no doubt.

We know that every life has meaning and that every life is worth protecting,

As president, I will always defend the first right in our Declaration of Independence—the right to life.

We issued a new proposal to prohibit Title Ten taxpayer funding from going to any clinic that performs abortions.

We are supporting the loving choice of adoption and foster care, including through the support of faith-based adoption services. And I am supporting the U.S. Senate's effort to make permanent the Hyde Amendment, which prohibits taxpayer funding for abortion in spending bills.

Today I have signed a letter to Congress to make clear that if they send any legislation to my desk that weakens the protection of human life, I will issue a veto. And we have the support to uphold those vetoes…each person is unique from Day One. That is a very important phrase. Unique from Day One. And so true…[32]

That philosophy is beneficial to black Americans, especially the black unborn. Obama's was definitely not. It was harmful to black women and their unborn children. Trump is just the opposite!

He made his position very clear in his February 5, 2019 State of the Union Address. Referring to pro-abortion laws and proposals in New York and Vermont:

There could be no greater contrast to the beautiful image of a mother holding her infant child than the chilling displays our nation saw in recent days. Lawmakers in New York cheered with delight upon the passage of legislation that would allow a baby to be ripped from the mother's womb moments before birth.

These are living, feeling, beautiful babies who will never get the chance to share their love and dreams with the world. And then, we had the case of the governor of Virginia where he stated he would execute a baby after birth. To defend the dignity of every person, I am asking the Congress to pass legislation to prohibit the late-term abortion of children who can feel pain in the mother's womb. Let us work together to build a culture that cherishes innocent life. And let us reaffirm a fundamental truth—all children—born and un-born—are made in the holy image of God.[33]

On January 23, 2020, President Trump became the first sitting U.S. presi-dent to attend the annual March for Life anti-abortion rally referenced above.

Cardinal Timothy Dolan, archbishop of New York, in an article in the February 8, 2019, *Wall Street Journal*, compared the unborn to how the Supreme Court in the infamous Dred Scott decision described slaves: "...not human...with no rights."[34] President Obama and his fellow Democrats and Progressives, including much of the black political and civil rights leadership, apparently feel the same way.

Ryan Bomberger of the Radiance Foundation hit the nail on the head in a February 4, 2019, article in Lifesitenews.com entitled "Democratic Party celebrates Black History Month by aborting more black babies." He wrote:

There is no situation, today, more emblematic of civil rights gone wrong than in the former Party of Slavery now proudly proclaiming its status of being the Party of Limitless Abortion. As someone who was once considered "black and unwanted" but adopted and loved instead, I pray that many in the black community will awaken and understand the dif-ference between being empowered and being fooled by those in power. Until then, the Democrat Party will keep pushing the horrific violence of abortion and making millions of blacks, history. I pray that many in the black community will awaken and understand the difference between being empowered and being fooled by those in power. Until then, the Democrat Party will keep pushing the horrific violence of abortion and making millions of blacks, history.[35]

Bomberg asks how many "millions need to be killed, harmed and exploited for Americans—of any hue—to wake up and see abortion for what it is: fatal systemic racism and elitism? The real shame is that Obama, and much of the black political and civil rights establishments, don't realize that by swimming in the abortion gutter and sewer with Planned Parenthood and the abortion lobby, that they are working against the interests of their own people!

By doing so, Obama and the other abortion cohorts have failed black America—Trump, by opposing abortion and supporting the sanctify of life is helping black Americans! As Kanye West said on Big Boy TV, "Democrats are....making us abort our children—Thou Shall Not Kill."[36]

CHAPTER 9
SCHOOL CHOICE

Trump Shows Commitment to Schools With DeVos Pick
Tuesday, November 29, 2016 09:33 AM

How ironic!

Blacks gave Barack Obama and the Democrats over 90 percent of their vote in 2008 and 2012 and got nothing in return to assist the plight of children trapped in inferior inner-city schools. Donald Trump got eight percent of the black vote and has already acted on his commitment to improve educational opportunities for those children — even though most of their parents probably supported Clinton!

Throughout the presidential campaign, Trump made bringing school choice to inner city parents a key part of his urban agenda. Speaking at a charter school in Cleveland, Ohio which serves mostly poor black children, he said that he was "proposing a plan to provide school choice to every disadvantaged student in America."

Trump's plan would direct $20 billion in federal education spending to school choice policies that would give students and their families the option of attending traditional public schools, public charter or magnet schools, or even private schools. His message: "As your president, I will be the nation's biggest cheerleader for school choice."

Within days of his election, Trump made good on his promise by naming school choice advocate Betsy DeVos to be secretary of education. DeVos, like Trump, believes that parents should have the ability to choose the best schools for their children, whether traditional public, charter, or private schools.

That's music to the ears of inner city and poor parents of all ethnic backgrounds.

By naming DeVos, Trump honored his commitment to improve inner city education right out of the gate. He has done more in a few weeks to improve the quality of education for low income children than Obama and Democrats have in decades.

They apparently care more about pleasing teachers' unions than the plight of poor inner-city kids.

Speaking of teachers' unions, guess how they reacted to Trump's appointment — certainly not as happy warriors!

The American Federation of Teachers (AFT) and the National Education Association (NEA), the unions that have done so much to provide us with high-quality inner-city schools — just kidding of course — were apoplectic over the DeVos appointment.

AFT president Randi Weingarten called DeVos "the most ideological, anti-public education nominee put forward since President Carter created a Cabinet-level Department of Education." Not to be out done, NEA president Lily Eskelsen García said DeVos has "lobbied for failed schemes, like vouchers — which take away funding and local control from our public schools — to fund private schools at taxpayers' expense."

Thankfully, these negative voices against greater educational opportunities for minority children — a unique form of liberal racism — will not prevail.

Beyond the group think bubble of progressive liberalism, in the real world, Trump's support of school choice and appointment of DeVos has many supporters.

Jeb Bush, who fought Trump bitterly during the GOP primaries, an education trailblazers in his own right, said that DeVos was "an outstanding pick" and that that her "allegiance is to families, particularly those struggling at the bottom of the economic ladder, not to an outdated public education model that has failed them from one generation to the next."

Bush, DeVos supporters, and conservatives throughout the country, will appreciate and most likely applaud the comments of incoming Florida House Speaker Rep. Richard Corcoran.

Commenting on the NEA's Florida counterpart, the Florida Education Association (FEA), Corcoran called it "downright evil" for its continued legal fight against Florida's tax credit scholarship program that provides low income families corporate-funded vouchers to attend private schools.

Adding a very refreshing and candid assessment of the group, he said the union was "attempting to destroy the lives of almost 100,000 children, mostly minority, and most of them poor" later saying to reporters the union actions were "disgusting" and "repugnant."

Cheers to the new speaker of the Florida House!

Corcoran, Bush and Trump are not the only ones supporting charter schools and choice for inner city parents.

In May, I wrote in this space how over 100 black ministers in Florida demonstrated at the state capital in Tallahassee urging the Florida NAACP to drop the lawsuit with the Florida teachers union — the same group Corcoran attacked — challenging the above-mentioned state tax credit program.

I quoted black newspaper and radio station owner R.B. Holmes, who said the NAACP was "on the wrong side of history."

The ministers weren't alone.

As I wrote then, "In January "nearly 11,000 private-school students, program supporters, school choice advocacy groups, and religious leaders went to Tallahassee in an over 240 bus convoy to ask the teachers union to drop its lawsuit. They argued that vouchers under the program were the only way for many families to escape under-performing schools."

I concluded saying that "Donald Trump should make it clear he stands with Florida's black ministers on this important issue . . . "

By appointing DeVos, he not only has made it clear that he stands with those black ministers — and Corcoran — but also with school choice advocates throughout the nation — including many in black America.

Obama Turned His Back on Inner-City Children

While Donald Trump has been a consistent supporter of school choice and vouchers for students from the beginning of his administration, as noted above, one of the first actions of Barack Obama was to end a successful District of Columbia School Voucher Program—the Opportunity Scholarship Program—which allowed students in the nation's capital to attend private schools.

The taxpayer-funded voucher program was enacted in 2004 by President George W. Bush and reauthorized in 2011.[37] The Opportunity Scholarship Program is the only federally funded private school choice program created by Congress. It allows students from low-income households an opportunity to have options outside the public schools in their neighborhood.

It initially started as a five-year pilot program in 2003 that provided a voucher with a value of up to $7,500 to about 1,700 students.

An April 2009, *U.S. News and World Report* editorial, "Obama Wrong on D.C. School vouchers and Hypocritical, Just Like Congress," quoted columnist and *Fox News* commentator Juan Williams writing that the decision to end the program was "Obama's outrageous sin against our kids." It further quoted him stating that improving big city education was the "key civil rights issue of this generation…If there is one goal that deserves to be held above day-to-day partisanship…it is the effort to end the scandalous poor level of academic achievement and abysmally high drop-out rates for America's black and Hispanic students."[38]

Then CNN commentator Ronald S. Martin—like Williams, also black—hit the nail on the head when he said that "preaching to the rest of us about the virtues of a public education, then sending your own children to private school and denying the use of vouchers so others can do the same is frankly hypocritical."[39]

Throughout his presidency, Obama tried to defund the successful DC voucher program which benefited over sixteen hundred low-income students, which had been revived thanks to then Republican Speaker of the House John Boehner, pressure from conservatives, and the parents of the students who were 99 percent black. Meanwhile, Obama sent his daughters to the prestigious Sidwell Friends School in Washington, DC.

For example, his 2015 $4 trillion budget, one of his last, provides a good example of his giving the cold shoulder to the educational aspirations of poor children in favor of teachers' unions. As *Investor Business Daily* editorialized at the time:

> This is one of the rare cases of a government program that actually works. The D.C. Opportunity Scholarship Program, as it is called, began under President George W. Bush in 2003 and has allowed thousands of children to enroll in private and Catholic schools by helping cover tuition costs, $8,000 to $10,000 a year.[40]

The editorial quoted Center for Education Reform President Kara Kerwin who said, "Every year since he has been president, Barack Obama has tried to shut down this education program. He just doesn't support private school choice."

Even more to the point was an opinion article in the February 8, 2015, *Washington Times* by the Heritage Foundation chief economist Stephen Moore. He wrote that Obama wanted to shut down private school choice because "teachers unions hate private school choice because many private school teachers aren't in the education union" and "the success of choice-based private schools in educating minorities and poor children gives public educators a big black eye because the kids do so much better with choice."

As Moore concluded:

> A quality education is the best anti-poverty program ever invented. This is the best path to reducing income inequality. Rich liberals would never condemn their own kids to rotten and dangerous inner-city public schools. Still, they force these schools on the poor and minorities they pretend

to care for. School choice, as Jack Kemp used to say, is the new civil rights issue in America.

Democrats are on the wrong side on this issue. They put unions ahead of kids.[41]

When it came to assisting poor and low-income students attend quality private or public schools of their choice, Obama failed black America!

Trump Solid on School Choice

In furtherance of his commitment to school choice, in 2017 the Trump administration reversed the Obama policy of denying vouchers and reinstated funding for low-income DC students to attend private schools.[42]

As noted earlier in the November 29 *Newsmax* article, which introduced this chapter, by naming DeVos Trump honored his commitment to improve inner city education right out of the gate: "He has done more in a few weeks to improve the quality of education for low income children than Obama and Democrats have in decades."

Since that time, he and his administration have worked to fulfill his goal of being "the nation's biggest cheerleader for school choice." In his February 5, 2019 State of the Union message, he told Congress that to "help support working parents, the time has come to pass school choice for America's children."[43]

In furtherance of the Trump school choice agenda, the President's 2020 Budget Request devoted significant resources to school choice programs as set forth below:[44]

1. INCREASE ACCESS TO SCHOOL CHOICE

President Trump believes that a child's future should not be determined by his or her parents' income or zip code. No child should be limited to a school that fails to meet his or her needs. Family access to a wide range of high-quality educational choices, including strong public, charter, magnet, private, online, parochial, and home school options must be expanded. Communities must be enabled to provide a robust range of schooling options, to ensure that all students can thrive in school and are prepared for success.

The fiscal year 2020 Budget Request includes proposals to expand school choice:

- $500.0 million for the Charter Schools Program, an increase of $60.0 million over the fiscal year 2019 appropriation, to support State and local efforts to establish new charter schools, replicate and expand existing high-performing charter schools, and help charter schools access high-quality facilities;

- $107.0 million for the Magnet Schools program, the same as the fiscal year 2019 appropriation, to increase educational options for students and families through the creation of high-quality magnet schools in local educational agencies (LEAs) implementing desegregation plans;

- $50.0 million for Student-Centered Funding Incentive Grants to help districts participate in flexibility agreements under Title I, Part E (Flexibility for Equitable Per-Pupil Funding) and implement more transparent funding systems where Federal, State, and local dollars follow each student; and

- Raising the Direct Student Services set-aside in Title I from 3 percent to 5 percent to encourage States to leverage more Title I funds to support public-school choice. A few States are already using this set-aside to allow students to take advantage of advanced coursework or career preparation classes not available in their assigned schools.

The President's 2020 Budget also would increase funding for the DC Opportunity Scholarship program which awards scholarships that allow K-12 students from low-income families in our Nation's capital to attend private schools.

Together, these policies create a comprehensive approach to providing all students—particularly disadvantaged students—with greater opportunities to attend a high-quality school. They are designed to focus education funds on the needs of students, rather than those of systems, school districts, or adults.

Note the reference to the DC Opportunity Scholarship program.

Education Freedom Scholarship Program

On September 16, Secretary DeVos kicked off her 2019 Back-to-School Tour in Milwaukee, Wisconsin, and Rockford, Illinois, schools to highlight the administration's Education Freedom Scholarship Program (EFS). The program will provide a $5 billion annual federal tax credit for voluntary donations to state-based scholarship programs and assist state and local school choice efforts.

The above Budget Message made specific reference to the EFS program:

The most transformative education proposal in the President's Budget Request is not a part of the Department of Education's fiscal year 2020 budget, but rather is proposed in the request for the Department of Treasury. It is a federal tax credit for voluntary donations to State-designed scholarship programs for elementary and secondary students, capped at $5.0 billion per year. This tax credit is available to individuals and domestic businesses. The donations will empower States to offer scholarships that can be used on a wide range of public and private educational activities. States, not the federal government, will determine family eligibility requirements and allowable uses of scholarship funds. Because it is a tax credit, it will not divert a single dollar away from public schools or teachers.

DeVos called the EFS program the most transformative idea for American education in decades.[45] Major highlights of the program include:

- Empowering students and families to choose the best educational setting for them—regardless of where they live, how much they make, and how they learn.

- Allowing families to receive and control the use of scholarships for their child's elementary and secondary education, which may include career and technical education, apprenticeships, and dual and concurrent enrollment.

- Providing privately funded scholarships that improve the educational experiences of students across the country, without taking a single dollar away from public schools and the students who attend them.

- Allowing individual and business taxpayers nationwide to contribute to student scholarships through state-identified Scholarship Granting Organizations (SGOs). Such contributions are eligible to receive a nonrefundable, dollar-for-dollar federal tax credit, but no contributor will be allowed a total tax benefit greater than the amount of their contribution.

- Expanding early learning, preschool, and career training options. [46]

These Trump school choice efforts are in stark contrast to Obama's inaction and outright hostility to any education programs or innovations opposed by the teachers' unions. While he—and his fellow Democrats—failed inner city and low-income black students in their quest for educational opportunity, Trump is helping them attain it.

Blacks' Support for School Choice Could Benefit Trump in 2020

If there is one issue that the Trump campaign can use in its reelection effort that would appeal to blacks, particularly black parents, it is school choice, including private-school vouchers and charter schools—and polls support that thesis.

A National School Choice Poll conducted by Beck Research for the American Federation of Children released in January of 2019 showed 63 percent support for school choice—including 73 percent from Latinos and "67 percent from African Americans."[47]

Evidence of how important school choice can be in close elections was shown clearly in the 2018 Florida governor's race.

I wrote in my *Newsmax* "Silent Minority" blog November 27, 2018, that, but for President Donald Trump's endorsement "and key support from black school-choice voters," Ron DeSantis probably would not be Florida's governor.[48]

The point was amplified in a November 20, 2018, *Wall Street Journal* article by William Mattox, who said that DeSantis owes his victory in Florida to about "100,000 African-American women who unexpectedly chose him over the black Democratic candidate Andrew Gillum."[49]

Mattox went on to write that in an election decided by "fewer than 40,000 votes, these 100,000 women proved decisive." He cited CNN's exit poll stating that of the 650,000 black women who voted, "18% chose" DeSantis. The point to be taken away is that, as Mattox stated, this support exceeds their support for Republican Senate candidate and former Governor

Rick Scott whom they gave only 9% and the 8% among black men and the GOP national average among black women of 7%."

Mattox says that the outcome of the Florida race "should encourage Republicans nation-wide to pitch their education agenda to minority voters."

He's right!

The question is whether Republicans and the Trump campaign will commit the resources to do it—especially in battleground states? It must reinforce what the *Wall Street Journal* concluded in its October 3, 2019, editorial: "The sad reality is that teachers unions run the public schools for themselves, not for the students."[50]

Historical Black Colleges and Universities

As outlined in this chapter, the president has been an ardent supporter of school choice, which is essential in expanding educational opportunities for students from low-income families. It is also necessary to mention the president's extensive support of Historically Black Colleges and Universities (HBCUs), which have been an essential factor in the creation of a black middle class.

As stated in the February 28, 2017, Presidential Executive Order cited below, HBCUs are located in 20 states, the District of Columbia, and the U.S. Virgin Islands; and, serve over 300,000 undergraduate, graduate, and professional students. The president's record on HBCU's is as remarkable as it has been on school choice including:

- Signing Executive Order 13779 that moved the federal initiative supporting HBCUs to the White House.

- Supporting and signing into law on December 19, 2019, H.R. 5363, the Future Act, which permanently extended mandatory funding for HCBU's.

- Restoring year-round Pell grants for low-income students and forgiving the debt of HBCU's that suffered damage from hurricanes Katrina and Rita.

Just as President Trump surpassed Barack Obama in supporting children trapped in under-performing inner-city schools, he also has far outpaced him on assisting HBCUs!

CHAPTER 10
URBAN REVITALIZATION

Obama Ignored Problems of Urban America

As I wrote in Chapter 4, Barack Obama basically ignored the problems of economic revitalization of inner cities except when forced to do so because of some racial incident.[51]

During his two terms, even when the Democrats controlled Congress for his first two years, there were no major legislative initiatives on jobs, reform of the juvenile and criminal justice systems, mandatory minimum sentencing, or other issues impacting young black and Hispanic males, including programs to crack down on gang violence! He had eight years to develop an urban agenda to deal with these and other issues.

Trump and Opportunity Zones

On December 22, 2017, President Trump signed the Tax Cuts and Jobs Act, which established Opportunity Zones[52] to incentivize long-term investments in low-income communities throughout the nation.

Opportunity Zones were an addition to the 2017 Tax Cuts and Jobs Act cosponsored by the Senate's only black Republican, Sen. Tim Scott (R-SC) with black Democrat Sen. Cory Booker (D-NJ). Pursuant to the Act, over 8,700 low-income census tracts called--Opportunity Zones—were created to spur economic development and job creation in distressed communities throughout the country and U.S. possessions by providing tax benefits to investors who invest eligible capital into these communities.

As outlined in the White House Fact Sheet, Opportunity Zones will "spur private-sector investment to revitalize hurting communities and unleash their economic potential…help drive economic growth and lift up communities that have been left behind."[53]

It described Opportunity Zones as a "powerful vehicle" for bringing economic growth and job creation to communities that need them most.

On average, the median family income in an Opportunity Zone is 37 percent below the state median; the average poverty rate is more than 32 percent, compared with a rate of 17 percent for the average US census tract; more than 8,760 communities in all fifty states, the District of Columbia, and five territories have been designated as Opportunity Zones; and nearly 35 million Americans live in communities so designated.

Scott told *Politico Money* that he had tried to create a program that creates an incentive for people to take a second look at parts of the country that have been "missed by the economic recovery experience over the last few years."[54] He went on to state that he believes the program could direct as much as $100 billion in investment to create jobs outside major metro areas that are already thriving.

White House Opportunity and Revitalization Council

To put the might of his entire administration behind Opportunity Zones, Trump signed Executive Order 13853 on December 12, 2018, establishing the White House Opportunity and Revitalization Council.[55] In signing the executive order, the president said that "52 million Americans" live in economically distressed communities. Moreover, he added, that despite the growing national economy, "these communities are plagued by high poverty levels, failing schools, and a scarcity of jobs."

The purpose of the council is to "carry out" the administration's plan to encourage public and private investment in urban and poor areas, including Opportunity Zones. The council is chaired by the Secretary of Housing and Urban Development, Dr. Ben Carson, and is composed of over fifteen federal agency heads or representatives. Among its tasks are the following:

- Engaging all levels of government to identify best practices and assist leaders, investors, and entrepreneurs in utilizing the Opportunity Zone incentive to revitalize low-income communities.

- Improving revitalization efforts by streamlining, coordinating, and targeting existing federal programs to economically distressed areas, including Opportunity Zones.

- Considering legislative proposals and undertaking regulatory reform to remove barriers to revitalization efforts.

- Presenting the president with a number of reports identifying and recommending ways to encourage investment in economically distressed communities.

Implementation Plan

In April of 2019, the White House released the council's "Implementation Plan" (Plan) outlining the council's plans to implement the reforms and initiatives that will "target, streamline, coordinate and optimize Federal resources in economically distressed communities to stimulate economic development, encourage entrepreneurship, expand educational and workforce development opportunities, and promote safe neighborhoods."[56]

The Plan takes note of the fact that, as previously mentioned, there are over 8,700 designated qualified Enterprise Zones in all fifty states, the

District of Columbia, and five US territories. Of those zones, 40 percent are located in rural census tracts, 38 percent in urban census tracts, and 22 percent in suburban census tracts.

The Plan outlines that the council will be composed of five subcommittees and work streams each with a lead agency:

Economic Development—Department of Commerce

Entrepreneurship—Small Business Administration

Safe Neighborhoods—Department of Justice

Education and Workforce Development—Departments of Labor and Education

Measurement—Council of Economic Advisers

These five work streams show that there is a recognition that the problems in economically depressed communities are impacted by a variety of factors, all of which have to be addressed if the accompanying investments are to be successful.

As an illustration, the Safe Neighborhoods work stream recognizes that crime and the "perception of unsafe neighborhoods are detriments to any revitalization effort." For example, in the 1980s, Secretary of Housing and Urban Development Jack Kemp was successful in attracting new business to distressed communities, but "high crime and lack of corresponding investment in public safety drove many businesses to leave." Addressing this aspect of the Plan is the responsibility of the Department of Justice which is prioritizing grant applications that provide resources in the zones for law enforcement, crime prevention, and victim services.

In education, it's no secret that distressed areas have major educational needs. As stated in the Plan, more than one-fifth of adults in economically distressed communities lack a high school diploma or equivalent. Accordingly, a main function of the Education and Labor Departments will include targeting "education and workforce development resources" to the zones and incentivizing "expansion of and investment in high-quality educational opportunities, especially charter schools," to serve students in the zones.

The Impact of Enterprise Zones and Supporting Efforts

The reason so much information has been provided on the Enterprise Zone program and the supporting efforts throughout the administration is that, in fewer than three years into his administration, Donald Trump has done more for neighborhood revitalization than Barack Obama did in eight.

This is just another area where Obama failed black America and Trump is helping!

CHAPTER 11

BLACKS AND THE TRUMP ECONOMY

Trump Repairing Obama's Economic Damage for Blacks and Hispanics

Thursday, July 11, 2019 05:59 PM

I am getting pretty fed up with the constant "fake news" barrage from Democrat presidential candidates and their fellow party and media sycophants arguing that Obama is responsible for the Trump booming economy.

What a lie.

BET founder and billionaire Robert Johnson said it well-- President Trump deserves credit for a "great" economy and low black unemployment.

"I think the economy is doing absolutely great, and it's particularly reaching into populations that heretofore had very bad problems in terms of jobs, unemployment and the opportunities that come with full employment, so African-American unemployment is at its lowest level."

He went on to say that he gives "the president a lot of credit for moving the economy in a positive direction that's benefiting a large amount of Americans" and "the tax cuts clearly helped."

The Wall Street Journal Editorial Board went even further in its July 4 editorial, "A Tale of Two Economies."

Among its excellent points:

- The jobless rate for blacks is 6.2%, which is only 2.9 percentage-points higher than for whites versus a 4.6 percentage-point difference before the start of the 2008 recession.

- Unemployment has fallen twice as much among blacks as whites since December 2016.

- Nearly one million more blacks and two million more Hispanics are employed than when Barack Obama left office.

- Minorities account for more than half of all new jobs created during the Trump Presidency.

- Unemployment among black women has hovered near 5% for the last six months, the lowest since 1972.

- A mere 3.5% of high school graduates are unemployed.

The editorial also disputes the allegation of presidential wannabee Sen. Kamala Harris, D-Ca, that people are "stringing jobs together to make ends meet." It points out that there are now "1.3 million fewer Americans working part time" for economic reasons than at the end of the Obama presidency.

Even more evidence of how the Trump economy has benefitted black and Hispanic Americans was pointed out in a July 8 Communications/Research Memo by Steve Guest, Rapid Response Director for the Republican Nation Committee, outlining how the Trump economy and polices "are helping workers more than Obama's did."

Among the significant points:

- "Wages are rising at the fastest rate in a decade for lower-skilled workers."

- "Unemployment among less-educated Americans and minorities is near a record low."

- "Nearly one million more blacks and two million more Hispanics are employed than when Obama left office."

- "Minorities account for more than half of all new jobs created during the Trump Presidency."

Guest rightly states in his "Bottom Line" that, "It is clear that the Democrat talking points on the economy are as phony as a $3 bill. President Trump's America First policies are delivering higher wages and lower unemployment for more Americans."

Trump's positive impact on the black economy is not the only issue on which Democrats are deceiving America. The citizenship question issue on the 2020 census is another.

House Speaker Nancy Pelosi, D-Ca., said that the president wanting to have a question on citizenship on the 2020 census is an effort to "Make America White Again." This is just another example of just how much she and Democrats' race baiting, like their false Obama economic claims, are out of touch with average Americans, especially blacks and Hispanics.

A Harvard University Center for American Political Studies/Harris poll found that 67% of all registered U.S. voters say the census should ask the citizenship question including 88% of Republicans, 63% of independents, 52% of Democrats, 74% of rural voters and most notably *59% of black and 55% of Hispanic voters.*

Pelosi and Democrats seem to think that fabricating economic facts, race-baiting, and a socialist agenda offers black and Hispanic Americans a political "Stairway to Heaven."

However, they will find that black and Hispanic voters will realize that the Democrats' "stairway" is nothing but a mirage and will see how Trump's economy is repairing the damage that Obama did to their communities.

Impeaching Trump Is Against Blacks' Economic Interests
Friday, September 27, 2019 04:23 PM

While black presidential candidates and their me-too black colleagues in the House of Representatives polish the impeachment boots of their white liberal Democrat and media establishment puppeteers, their black constituents are making historic gains in the Trump economy.

Two years ago, in an August 21, 2017, article in the Chicago Tribune, Heritage Foundation Senior Fellow, Trump campaign economic adviser, and nominee for the Federal Reserve Board Stephen Moore, said that Trump was creating "more jobs and higher incomes for blacks."

He also cited statistics showing that the black unemployment rate had fallen by a full percentage point; black labor force participation was up; and the number of black Americans with a job had risen by 600,000 from the prior year; and, that preliminary data showed black wages and incomes were up.

That was impressive two years ago!

Two years later, the economic plight of blacks is even better in the Trump economy. According to the Department of Labor's Bureau of Labor Statistics, the average August unemployment rate for blacks — for 2017, 2018, and 2019 — was 6.5 percent.

That includes the August 2019 black unemployment rate, released September 6, of 5.5%. As Black Enterprise Magazine reported, it was the lowest rate recorded since the Labor Department began tracking the progress back in the 1970's!

As a September 20, 2019, Wall Street Journal (WSJ) editorial pointed out, citing the then-latest Census Bureau and Labor Department numbers:

- The greatest employment gains for full-time year-round workers in 2018 were among minority female-led households including a 4.2 percentage point increase among blacks.

- The poverty rate among female households declined 2.7 percentage points for blacks.

- The jobless rate for black women in August fell to 4.4% — an historic low.

In addition to that positive news, the WSJ also reported that a New York Federal Reserve Board national survey showed that the unemployment rate among Americans without a high-school diploma has fallen "steeply over the past three years, and the rate for black women fell in August to the lowest level on record."

Regarding his record on blacks, Trump summed it up nicely in a September 2018 tweet. He cited the economic and "other things" he had done and asked: "…how do Democrats, who have done NOTHING for African-Americans but TALK, win the Black Vote?"

The same question can be asked today.

Trump is helping blacks economically as noted above, and educationally through support for school choice and historically black colleges and universities.

It could be argued that the black presidential candidates and their black friends in the House of Representatives, and the four Congresswomen known as the "Squad", have done little if anything for blacks — economically or educationally.

They want to get rid of a president who is doing more to assist their black and Hispanic constituents in those key areas than they, or Barack Obama, ever did. Hopefully it will be noticed.

An August 2016 Gallup poll showed that 52% of blacks said that Obama's policies had not gone far enough in helping the black community, up from 20% during the 2008 campaign and 32% his first year in office.

Just as a majority of blacks were cognizant of the fact that Obama had not done enough for the black community after eight years, they also will know that these black Democrats are not serving their interests.

Jumping aboard the "Impeachment Express" as it stops at the Democrat plantation might be in the political interests of the black political elite, but it is not in the best interests of black Americans and their children who are benefiting under Trump's economic, educational, and other policies.

The Good News Continues

Since Bob Johnson's comments noted above in July, he has reiterated his praise of the impact of the Trump economy on blacks. Speaking on CNBC's *Squawk Box* in September, Johnson said that the economic trends for blacks "continues to be favorable." To make his point, Johnson referred an old saying that "When White America catches a cold, African Americans get pneumonia." He stated that it's going the "opposite way now. White unemployment is going down, African American unemployment is going down. That's a plus-plus that you can't argue with."[57]

Supporting Johnson's view was the Bureau of Labor Statistics March 6, 2020 Job Report showing that the unemployment rate for black Americans, which hit a record low of 5.4 percent in August, averaged a still low 5.6 percent the last quarter of 2019.[58]

Regarding the poverty rate, according to the U.S. Census Bureau September 10, 2019 report on income and poverty in the United States in 2018, overall and for blacks, the picture is also a positive for Trump's economy.[59] The official poverty rate in 2018 was 11.8 percent down from 12.3 percent in 2017—a .5 percentage point decrease. For blacks, the corresponding rates were 20.8 percent and 21.2 percent respectively, a .4 percentage point decrease. For the first time in eleven years, the official poverty rate was significantly lower than 2007, the year before the most recent recession.

On household income, the report stated that in 2018 the median household income for blacks was listed as $41,361 versus $40,324 in 2017, an increase of $1,037.

As to food stamps, since December of 2016, the last month of the Obama administration, and November of 2019, nearly seven million people left the food stamp program based on U.S. Department Agriculture Food and Nutrition Service information.[60] Participation reached the highest levels in the history of the program during the Obama administration with average participation peaking at over 47 million in fiscal year 2013.[61] For blacks, during that peak year, black participation reached 12.1 million[62] and dropped in fiscal 2017 to 10.5 million—a decrease of 1.6 million.[63]

These statistics show that black America has not lost, but has gained, in the Trump economy.

Trump's Economic Tide Is Lifting Many Boats

The economic data in this chapter clearly illustrates that the maxim "A rising tide lifts all boats" certainly applies to black Americans. Blacks are not the only beneficiaries. The Trump economic tide has lifted the boats of millions of other Americans as well, and Americans agree. According to a December CNN poll, 76 percent of those polled rated the economy very or somewhat good—the highest percentage since 2001—including 97 percent of Republicans, 75 percent of independents, and 62 percent of Democrats.[64]

Rising Black Household Income

The above statistics are not the only evidence that the Trump economy and policies are benefiting black Americans. An October report by the liberal Brookings Institution, "Black household income is rising across the United States," found that among the top five US metropolitan areas with the largest black populations, there were significant increases in median black household incomes from 2013 through 2018.[65]

In the New York metro area, the increase was 14.6 percent; Atlanta, 20.8 percent; Chicago, 11.3 percent; Dallas, 12.2 percent; and Washington, DC, 7.1 percent. The report also notes that the metro areas in the West and South recorded the largest statistical increases in black media household incomes, with San Francisco and Seattle topping the list with increases of 36.4 percent and 30.8 percent more in 2018 than in 2013, respectively.

Other metro areas with significant income gains in that period were Phoenix, Arizona (28.9 percent); Riverside, California (26.9 percent); Tampa, Florida (21.8 percent); and Orlando, Florida (21.6 percent).

What accounts for these positive changes? The report said that one likely factor is "employment opportunity." It stated that there was a "positive, significant association between the change in Black employment rates and Black median household incomes across the metro areas from 2013 to 2018."

The Democrats and the Congressional Black Caucus would have you believe that any improvement in the economy, decrease in black unemployment, and increase in median household income of black households is because Trump "inherited" Obama's economy.

Not quite!

There is no way the economic gains we have seen since the president came into office would have occurred with the Obama and Democrats' "tax, spend, and regulate" philosophy of government. The success we have seen is because of the president's—not Obama's—economic policies. A few are set forth below.

A December 16, 2019, White House fact sheet outlined several accomplishments of the president's economic policies. These include the addition of more than seven million jobs; the unemployment rate falling to 3.5 percent, a fifty-year low; annual nominal wages growing by 3 percent in 2019 for the first time in a decade; and wage growth being higher for lower-income workers compared to higher-income workers, workers compared to managers, and black Americans compared to white Americans.[66]

The fact that wages for the typical worker—nonsupervisory employees who account for a majority of the workforce—are rising at the fastest rate in more than a decade is a sign that the labor market has tightened. That means many black Americans are better off financially than they were under Obama.

Just look at a few of the indicators of how Trump policies are benefiting black Americans.

The Stock Market

The stock market reached record highs during 2019. The Dow Jones Industrial Average, the S&P 500, and Nasdaq all had record gains under President Trump, rising 22.3 percent, 28.9 percent, and 35.2 percent, respectively.[67] The left wants to downplay the significance of this by saying only the wealthy are in the stock market. Not true.

As we all know, many more Americans of every race are in the stock market as corporations phase out of pension plans and replace them with 401(k) plans invested in the exchanges. Workers of all races in state and local public employee union funds are also benefitting because their pension funds invest significantly in the stock market. Therefore, millions of black Americans on Main Street are reaping the rewards of robust action on Wall Street and have been better off since Donald Trump took office.

Cutting Federal Regulations

It's not talked about much, but Trump's reduction in the scope and cost of federal regulations has been an essential ingredient in the increase in new jobs, rising wages, and low unemployment discussed above. Unnecessary and burdensome regulations hurt business because they make it harder to do business.

This is especially true for small and minority businesses at the state and local levels. The young black man who wants to open a barbershop or black woman who wants to start a cake catering company selling her grandma's signature red velvet cake does not need burdensome regulations and licensing rules as impediments to going into business. That's why the administration's "Governors' Initiative on Regulatory Innovation" to work with state and local governments on advancing occupational licensing reform and cut regulations at the local level is so essential.[68]

Obama famously asked in 2016, "What magic wand " did Trump have to bring manufacturing jobs back to the United States?[69] Trump's "magic wand" turned out to be his belief in the American worker, investment in American ingenuity, and implementation of policies such as those discussed in this section, resulting in hundreds of thousands of new manufacturing jobs.

Tax Cuts

Another area where Obama's liberal minions, Progressives, the mainstream media, and many of the Democratic presidential candidates continually criticize Trump is on his tax cuts created by the Tax Cuts and Jobs Act (TCJA) two years ago. Those cuts continue to fuel this booming Trump economy. According to the president's Council of Economic Advisers, American businesses have repatriated $1 trillion in past overseas earnings previously invested abroad back home from overseas.[70]

Among other things, the act brought much-needed tax relief to American small businesses and boosted disposable income for most households. It also created Opportunity Zones to spur investment in economically depressed areas discussed in chapter 10.

Does anyone who is in the real world believe that the Obama administration or a successor Hillary Clinton administration would have cut taxes and slashed cumbersome federal regulations?

No way!

Democrats and their friends in the Obama media won't tell you this, but the economic gains since Trump took office, many of which are listed above, are because of his economic policies—not Obama's.

Barack Obama may have been the first president who shared the same skin color as his fellow black Americans. However, it is Donald Trump whose economic and social policies are benefiting black Americans.

Black Political and Civil Rights Leadership Silent on Black Progress Under Trump

With the positive economic performance of the Trump economy as outlined in this chapter and its positive impact on black Americans, one would think that the black civil rights and political leadership would at least give the president some credit. Don't hold your breath!

I wrote in June of 2018 that black leadership was "shamefully silent" on Trump's record on employment, notwithstanding the then-record-low 5.9 percent black unemployment rate.[71]

As I stated, if "Obama had overseen an economy with under 6 percent black unemployment, the CBC, mainstream media and the National Association for the Advancement of Colored People (NAACP), would be 'delirious.'

With Trump's record low numbers, they still remain silent—except to criticize!

After CBC members voted unanimously to impeach the president, and in spite of all of the economic and social policies outlined in this and previous chapters, it issued a press release stating in part:

> Black people have lost a lot since President Trump was sworn into office. The list of regressive and racist policies proposed by Donald Trump's administration is long and sad. To add insult to injury…he has never championed a single policy or program for Black people.[72]

What a major statement of fantasy and fiction! Where have they been living? I guess they think that the president's efforts and championing of the First Step Act and criminal justice reform, Opportunity Zones, and school choice are "regressive and racist" and are not important for black people. By making such false statements, they are deceiving black Americans--especially those they are supposed to represent--who are benefiting from these and other aspects of the Trump economy.

That's because the CBC, most of the black political, academic, and media establishments are apologists for the Democratic Party. The civil rights leadership, such as the NAACP, Reverend Jesse Jackson's Rainbow Coalition and Reverend Al Sharpton's National Action Network, are adjuncts of the Democrat Party. It will snow in the Sahara Desert before any of these groups or their leaders dare commend Donald Trump for anything positive that he does for black Americans. For example, there was no rush by any of these groups to commend him for his efforts on the First Step Act or Opportunity Zones initiatives, even though blacks will be among the main beneficiaries.

The reason is simple.

One of the founding principles of the CBC when formed in 1971, was expressed by William "Bill" Clay Sr., (D-MO): "Black people have no permanent friends, no permanent enemies…just permanent interests."[73]How things have changed!

Since the CBC was formed, the leadership of the black political and civil rights establishments have become "overseers" of the black "Democratic Plantation." They are joined at the hip with that party and its failed educational, economic, and urban policies.

They have adopted that party and its allies as "permanent friends" whose interests are their "permanent interests." They dare not leave that "plantation" whose policies they are loath to criticize.

The role and impact of these overseers and their "closed political minds" and incestuous relationship with the Democrats have been and are mainly responsible for many of the problems facing black America for over five decades.

That's why the silence on Trumps' successes. The role of these so-called leaders and overseers is explored in Part III of this book, "Epilogue."

Part II Conclusion

As I wrote in chapter 5, "What Do You Have To Lose," Trump inflamed the black political and media establishments in a speech near Milwaukee in 2016 when he told the truth about how the Democratic Party has failed and "betrayed the African-American-community and that its crime, education, and economic policies have produced only more crime, more broken homes, and more poverty." His words echo throughout our urban areas to this day:

> There is no compassion in allowing drug dealers, gang members, and felons to prey on innocent people…It is the first duty of government to keep the innocent safe and . . .

> I will fight for the safety of all Americans, especially those Americans who have not known safety for a very, very long time. [74]

The statistics and related information in Part II show that Trump was right and that black America has not lost, but has gained, in the Trump economy and from his policies in three short years in the key areas of immigration, criminal justice reform, school choice, urban revitalization, respect for the sanctity of human life and the unborn, and the economy.

Much could be and has been written on the failures of Barack Obama—who prided himself in being a "community organizer"—to make solving the problems of urban America a priority of his administrations. Obviously, he did not. As noted in the Introduction, the purpose of this book was *not* to do an exhaustive treatise on those failures. Rather, the purpose was to focus on a few key areas as noted in Part I and contrast those failures to President Trump's successes in those areas as set forth in Part II.

Coronavirus Update

The information in this chapter regarding the Trump economy and its benefits to black America is reflective of the economic environment before the Coronavirus (COVID-19) pandemic. Just as blacks were reaping the benefits of a booming economy, the virus shut the country down.

As Robert (Bob) Johnson is quoted as saying earlier in this chapter: "When White America catches a cold, African Americans get pneumonia." The virus, as the president has noted, is having a disproportionate impact on black Americans. Thousands who work in major department stores, hospitality, travel, restaurant, and other industries lost their jobs because of the pandemic.

Unfortunately, many who refused to give the president credit for the phenomenal pre-pandemic economy used the pandemic for political purposes. They blamed him for not acting fast enough even though he had restricted travel from China—a move many of his critics derided as unnecessary and xenophobic.

Dr. Anthony Fauci, director of the National Institute of Allergy and Infectious Diseases (NIAID) at the National Institutes of Health (NIH)—and member of the president' Coronavirus Task Force—disagreed. He said that the Trump administration' early decision banning travel from China slowed the spread of the virus.

Despite such politically biased criticism, the president showed exemplary leadership. He directed the marshaling of federal and private sector resources to fight a war against the virus. The mission was to bring relief to those who lost revenue and jobs in the greatest crisis facing America since World War II.

The president sought and received from Congress an initial historic $2 billion stimulus package. It included loans to small businesses, direct payments to individuals, and increased unemployment benefit assistance to battle the economic impact of the pandemic.

The goal of the president's COVID-19 effort and policies was to return to the reinvigorated Trump economy outlined in this chapter. Without the gains and cushion of that economy, the economic damage to black Americans and the country would have been much worse!

PART III:

EPILOGUE

CHAPTER 12

HISTORICAL PERSPECTIVE

Failed Black Leadership—Nothing Has Changed

The reader will note that a consistent theme in many of the *Newsmax* articles in this book is how the black political and civil rights leadership has historically failed the black community by being an echo chamber for the Democratic Party and the liberal establishment on virtually all issues. The same can be said of much of the black journalism community.

This is not a recent phenomenon and was the subject of my first published article in 1983 in the *Washington Times* and a subsequent article in *Human Events Online* in 2001 reflecting the same theme.

The *Washington Times* article was entitled "The closed minds of black Leaders." The full-page commentary was well received and discussed how the black leadership was in bed with the Democrat liberal establishment. The essence of the article was captured nicely in the editorial cartoon showing caricatures of "civil rights leaders" in bed with "Democrats," "labor," and the "NEA" (National Education Association) with the caption: "Yes, but will you still respect us in the morning?"

The *Human Events* article, "Monopoly of the Black Overseers" concludes: "Will the 'overseers' and their liberal allies keep their black flock behind the gates of the liberal plantation for the next twenty-one years? Or will a new generation of black voters and leaders finally bring political emancipation?"

The answer today, nineteen and thirty-seven years after the *Human Events* and *Washington Times* articles, respectively, were written, is that nothing has really changed— the "overseers" continue to keep their black flock behind the gates of the "liberal plantation." A clear example is set forth in my January 7, 2020 *Newsmax* article, "Black Caucus Deceives Blacks on Trump," which follows the *Washington Times* and *Human Events* articles.

If anyone doubted my references to the "Black Democrat Plantation" and 'liberal plantation" in this book, look no further than what happened to State Representatives Karen Whitsett of Michigan and Vernon Jones of Georgia—both black Democrats.

On April 14, 2020, Whitsett had the gall to thank the president at the White House for her recovery from the COVID-19 virus after taking a drug that he had mentioned as possibly being beneficial to treating the infection. Michigan Democrats censured her for expressing appreciation to the president on this critical issue!

Jones praised and endorsed the president for his record on job creation, supporting black colleges, and prison sentence reform. The backlash, including threats to him and his family, caused him to consider leaving the Democratic Party. According to an April 22, 2020 *Atlanta Journal-Constitution* article, Jones said in a statement: "Turn the lights off, I have left the plantation." The paper reported the next day that he had changed his mind saying in a Twitter video that he would not "now allow the Democrats to bully me into submission. I will not let them win. I will NOT resign."

These are two excellent examples of why "Nothing has Changed!"

THE WASHINGTON TIMES
COMMENTARY
THURSDAY, AUGUST 4, 1983

The closed minds of black leaders
CLARENCE V. MCKEE

Vice President George Bush has a civil rights record that ranks among the best of any person in public office, Republican or Democrat. However, given the discourteous treatment afforded him by the leadership and delegates to the NAACP convention in New Orleans, none of that seemed to matter.

Said a headline in *The Washington Post* "Bush Booed by Delegates at NAACP Session." "Bush Jeered by Blacks," said *The New York Times*. A *Los Angeles Times* story said, "Even the organist showed partiality, playing a rousing tune when former Democratic Vice President Mondale finished his speech and funeral music after Republican Vice President Bush quit the lectern."

How did NAACP Executive Director Benjamin Hooks react? After spending an entire week whipping the delegates into an emotional anti-Reagan, anti-Republican frenzy, Hooks said: "I applaud the delegates for sitting there listening to what they didn't want to hear."

What the delegates did not want to hear was Bush telling the truth. As he said, blacks are "taken for granted, marching lock step" with the Democratic Party. He should have known the NAACP. a so-called "non-partisan" organization, has dedicated itself to defeating Ronald Reagan and did not want to be "fair" or "look at the record and not the rhetoric."

He also should have known that, for the NAACP and in most quarters of black civil-rights leadership, there are no "open minds" when it comes to the administration's efforts and commitments to solving some of the crucial problems facing black Americans.

It was quite a show of demagoguery in New Orleans. Hooks, in his Tuesday keynote address, challenged President Reagan to a dialogue with black Americans and had the audience cheering and applauding. From then on, the NAACP leadership laid a very nice foundation of anti-Reaganism during the convention and continuously reiterated its top priority: defeat Reagan.

On Friday, the scene was orchestrated so that Bush appeared following Democratic presidential candidates who poured on more anti-Reagan gasoline, igniting it with the "I will appoint more blacks, Reagan is horrible, and I love the black and the poor" rhetoric that such groups seem to love hearing.

It is simply amazing that the president's and vice president's advisers have not learned that there is nothing they or anyone can do to curry favor or placate the major civil-rights leaders and their organizations. They are basically in "step" with and in apparent sympathy with the Democratic Party, and whoever else comes along to tell them." I love the black and the poor."

The time has come to be candid in stating that the Reagan administration and the Republican National Committee should not waste their energy going to these conventions. They should be attending and presenting their message to gatherings of more objective and politically neutral black organizations. Which ones? How about the National Bar Association, the National Medical Association, the Elks and the Links? And the major fraternities and sororities? And black church groups and gatherings of the black press?

That the GOP has not been establishing effective dialogues with these groups is one of the major problems Republicans have. They don't seem to know how to develop an effective counterattack to Democratic demagoguery or heed the advice of their own black appointees on how to do so. Just as liberal whites during the '60s seemed to enjoy having black-power advocates berate and belittle them as "honkies," "whitey," and "devils" at receptions and conventions, 1983 Republican leaders seem to enjoy being told how bad they are and they don't fight back.

It is ironic that the same NAACP which was so vociferous and self-righteous toward Bush had only weeks earlier stripped of authority the only major black female power-broker in the civil-rights community. When Margaret Bush Wilson was rebuked and humiliated by a mostly all-male NAACP board of directors there was not one public peep from the women of the NAACP or from those liberal feminists and ERA proponents of the National Organization of Women or the National Women's Political Caucus, most of whom had just lambasted Reagan in San Antonio over his alleged poor treatment of women.

I remember the 1980 Republican Platform affirmed that "Republicans will not make idle promises to blacks and other minorities: we are beyond the day when any American can live off rhetoric or political platitudes... Nor are we prepared," said the platform statement, "to accept the practice of turning the poor into permanent wards of the state, trading their political support for continued financial assistance."

The NAACP and most of the Democratic-leaning national black leadership apparently reject this view since they continue to demand more of the same rhetoric and platitudes from Democratic candidates.

Granted, most of the elected blackpolitical leadership is Democratic, so it's understandable they would do everything possible to see that any Reagan initiative to solve some basic problems is ignored, criticized or ridiculed. That's the stuff of partisan politics. However, the non-elected black leadership should not have the same party loyalty and subjectivity when it comes to the basic survival of over 12 percent of the nation's population. The record and facts show that this is not the case.

In 1980, inflation, high interest rates, crime and a stagnating economy were taking a disproportionate toll in black communities throughout the nation. However, most of black leadership followed Jimmy Carter.

He and his black surrogates implied that Reagan was a racist; they promised more federal programs. The result -- blacks gave the Democrats over 90 percent of their vote. Although the Democrats lost the White House and the Senate, black leadership continued to stay in the same bed and looked for every opportunity to attach and criticize the new Republican administration and its initiatives.

In 1983, the same black leaders, some of whom unfortunately oppose a black presidential bid, are once again ready to give all to the Democratic Party. Once again, the "rhetoric" and "platitudes" condemned in the GOP platform appear more important than having an honest debate over alternative solutions to pressing problems.

The sad part is that black leadership and the Democratic Party, except for affirmative action, have all but forgotten the foundation of black America -- *the black middle class.*

By not honestly addressing Reagan initiatives, and continuing to refer to black voters as "the black and the poor" they ignore important and pressing concerns in education, jobs and basic community survival with which such blacks must deal every day.

The black middle class produces the leaders of groups such as the NAACP, Urban League and various professional organizations. It is to this group that poor blacks look for role models and direction. What issues face this group of forgotten people who work as teachers, policemen, doctors, lawyers, businessmen, secretaries and government employees, and many of whom must work two jobs to make ends meet?

In education, the NAACP and much of the black leadership oppose Reagan's proposals to provide tuition-tax credits to parents who want to send their children to private schools. This is not a plan to destroy the public-school system. Indeed, this program would give needed competition to the public-education monopoly led by the National Education Association, which also sleeps in the Democratic Party bed.

A study by the Joint Center for Political Studies says 47 percent of 17-year-old blacks are illiterate. This report, by black professionals, says "public education has become an instrument for blocking rather than facilitating mobility." Yet most of black leadership opposes tuition-tax credits.

It's unfair to tell a poor, lower or middle-class black parent struggling to provide a quality education for his or her child that that 10-year-old son or daughter must wait five to 10 years while the public schools improve instead of taking any immediate opportunity to get that child into a quality education structure. Opposition to tax credits helps the education establishment but does it help the black child when he graduates not being able to read, write or articulate?

The same hypocrisy prevails in the area of neighborhood revitalization, another key component of the 1980 GOP Platform. While most black leaders attach the president for the lack of jobs and stagnation in black communities, the president's Enterprise Zone proposal has been buried in the

Democratic-controlled House without even being given a hearing. It has, however, passed the Republican-controlled Senate.

Do those same black leaders attack Tip O'Neill and Democratic committee chairmen for holding up this important legislation which could provide incentives to companies to move into inner-city areas to create jobs and training opportunities? Of course not.

These same leaders, for the most part, join with organized labor, another auxiliary of the Democratic Party, in opposing the administration's proposal for a youth minimum wage whereby young people could be hired by employers at less than the current minimum wage in order to encourage the hiring of more teenagers.

When black teen-age unemployment is at disastrously high levels in our cities, it would seem that the same leadership which attacks the administration on that issue would do all that it could to implement or at least discuss the sub-minimum wage proposal. However, the AFL-CIO, which provides financial assistance to many of these groups and many black elected officials, would be most upset if any of the leadership supported the concept.

Can you think of more pressing issues in the inner cities than black-on-black crime, drug trafficking, the deplorable statistics on black teenage pregnancy and increasing abortions? Yet, the NAACP boos and hisses the vice president, who only weeks earlier had announced a major administration initiative on drug interdiction to fight drug trafficking. While the NAACP berates the President of the United States and takes away the power of its own first lady, Mrs. Wilson, first lady Nancy Reagan has launched her own personal crusade against drug and alcohol abuse among youth. And the administration has sought a tougher federal criminal code.

Does black leadership or the NAACP acknowledge such efforts and inform the black population of what is being done in this area? Of course not.

Meanwhile, millions of black poor and middle-class parents fear the time when their child will become a victim of drugs, alcohol abuse or teen-age crime. Do the Democratic candidates for the presidency talk about these issues? Of course not. They know that all that is required to placate and appease black audiences is the same old rhetoric.

Black parents want to see their children score high on SAT and other important standardized tests and to get the best education possible. Black leadership, however, is more concerned with having a black child in a classroom with white children through forced busing than in urging its allies in the educational establishment to start teaching children how to read and write and supporting merit pay and accountability for teachers and principals.

The District of Columbia school system, with dedicated leadership and direction from its superintendent and with the support of local elected officials, has shown that a predominantly black urban school system can produce results. Those same leaders who criticize the president and join with Democratic candidates in urging billions more for education ignore the fact that even with billions in the past, our educational system has grossly short-changed black children. They offer no new alternatives in public. However, in private they, too, ask why so many black students and star college athletes can not speak proper English.

Probably the greatest tragedy is that black political leaders refuse to acknowledge that black people buy homes, cars, household appliances and seek bank loans and credit where high interest rates and double-digit inflation, caused by the Democratic programs of the past, have served to cripple their ability to provide basic necessities for their families.

They just will not admit that the economic recovery which has produced increased auto sales and lower interest rates not only has allowed unemployed black auto workers and employees of subsidiary industries to return to work, but also has allowed lower — and middle--income blacks to purchase automobiles and other basic needs. Not to admit that Reagan efforts to rejuvenate the economy will assist black people is most unfortunate. Of course, in good times, there would be very little to attack and hence posturing and yelling at the president would not gain as many headlines or be so well received among black masses. In a strong economy, many black people might just have enough money left over to make a contribution to the very same civil-rights organizations that now criticize the administration one day and seek federal, union and charitable funds the next day because not enough of their people have either the money or interest to support their organizations.

It is time for black ministers, the black press, and black professional organizations to reassume the leadership of black America they long ago turned over to civil-rights leaders and politicians. *There is simply no system of checks and balances in the black leadership establishment.* There *is no debate, discussion or even spirited argument over alternative solutions to many of the problems affecting black Americans.*

The problems that touch poor black Americans are sometimes different from those affecting middle-class blacks. Although the underlying current of racial discrimination is ever-present for all blacks, it is time to admit that there are different problems which require different solutions. The time when all blacks are lumped together as "black and poor" by Democrats and black leadership must end. It serves no purpose other than the aims of the Democratic Party and its allies who exploit black Americans for their own gain, power and position.

It is also time for black leadership to take a second look at all those "liberal" groups which say they are allies of black people. While black leaders used to speak in terms of the needs and problems of blacks, current black leadership seems most anxious to be friends to every other group that comes along such as feminists, gays, unions and the teaching establishment, as well as those who oppose nuclear weapons, the military and a strong US foreign policy. For credibility, such groups seek out blacks and create a situation where black leaders can't discuss black problems without including "other minorities, women, and gays" in the same sentence.

The result is that those groups are slowly co-opting blacks to get the attention of the press and politicians.

How have black concerns been co-opted? A recent meeting of the nation's mayors gave major attention to a demand that the federal government provide $50 million to combat AIDS. This disease does pose a serious problem. But crime, drugs, poor education and neighborhood revitalization are more important issues in most cities with large black populations. The request was a blatant appeal to the growing political power of the so-called "gay" movement to the exclusion of black constituencies at a time when the results of a 1979-81 study show a black infant-mortality rate 50 percent higher than that for whites in 32 of 45 cities; double the rate for whites in

15 cities, and in 1979, was 91 percent higher than the white rate nationally -- a 30 percentage-point increase over the 1950 figure.

As long as Ronald Reagan and the Republican Party are made scapegoats for all problems affecting blacks, the Democratic Party and much of the civil-rights leadership will continue to monopolize the minds and politics of the American black population and offer the same solutions, rhetoric and platitudes. Also, until the Republican Party and blacks with a different perspective begin fighting back, nothing will change.

Although the GOP can win the White House with little or no black support, it also can lose the Senate and scores of state and local legislators, mayors and governors with a massive black Democratic turnout in 1984.

Hence, just as the GOP cannot ignore black voter power at the state and local level and must begin fighting back, black leadership cannot ignore that most problems blacks face have not and will not be solved by Democratic promises of more of the same. Time is running out. While most black civil-rights leaders jump aboard the Democrats' "Defeat Reagan Express", few seem to be boarding the "Save The Children" local."

HUMAN EVENTS-ONLINE

End Monopoly of Black Overseers
By Clarence V. McKee
THE WEEK OF APRIL 30, 2001

In last November's election, the established "black leadership" once again delivered over 90% of the black vote to the Democratic presidential candidate.

There should be no doubt that much of the black civil rights and political leadership has become wholly owned subsidiaries of the Democratic Party and the liberal Democratic establishment. They react to the call of labor unions, abortion-on-demand feminists, and other members of the liberal Democratic coalition. As "overseers" of the "black political plantation" for the liberal establishment, the civil rights coalition, most of the legislative Black Caucuses, and scores of blacks in journalism and academia serve as advocates for a one-sided liberal viewpoint.

For years they have led their flock to feed at the Democratic Party trough as if it were a political "Promised Land." They are true soldiers in the liberal establishment's army.

If the black vote were taken out of the voting statistics, George Bush would have received a solid majority of the popular vote. According to the Joint Center for Political and Economic Studies and the Voter News Service, President Bush received 54% of the white vote. In Florida, where the black share of the vote grew 50%—from 10% to 15%—between 1996 and 2000, blacks delivered 93% of their votes to Al Gore. But Gore lost, and Democrats still do not control either the U.S. or Florida house or senate.

After their massive political defeat, that same leadership continues to direct postelection attacks on Florida with cries of "disenfranchisement," "illegitimacy" and "racism." Notwithstanding the fact that there was and is no firm proof that the election machinery—mostly controlled by Democrats at the local level—systematically disenfranchised black voters, they persist with their charges. Their loose rhetoric fosters disillusion and distrust of the voting process among black youth. Most important, their "all eggs in one Democratic political basket" strategy has effectively locked their followers out of the power corridors of the executive and legislative branches of government both nationally and in Florida.

They refuse to acknowledge the fact that their massive voter registration and turnout effort did not include educating many of these new black voters on the ballot process. As the Tampa *Tribune* recently suggested, the problem with many of these first-time voters was the inability to read and understand ballot instructions. Whether the national liberal establishment, black leadership and apparently partisan U.S. Civil Rights Commission will acknowledge this fact remains to be seen. It is more likely that their real goal is to embarrass Florida Gov. Jeb Bush and harm his chances for reelection.

When members of the Congressional Black Caucus staged a "protest" over Florida's electoral votes, not one Democratic U.S. senator joined them—not even the most liberal of the liberals. They got smiles and scattered applause but no support.

The sad fact is that the black leadership rarely gets anything in return for being the cannon fodder for the liberal left. Notwithstanding the 90% support and the fact that many senators would not have won but for the black vote, the black leadership was unable to get former Atlanta Mayor Maynard Jackson installed as chairman of the Democratic National Committee. Remaining blind to its impotence within the Democratic liberal establishment, this leadership is now demanding that President Bush "reach out" to the black community whose leaders through the NAACP ran vicious race-baiting ads trying to link him to the dragging death of a black man in Texas.

When a Republican or a conservative does reach out to assist black Americans, his good deeds are rarely praised and are often distorted. Atty. Gen. John Ashcroft had a commendable record of appointing blacks in Missouri, but, when the order went out to "Bork" him, those in the Missouri black community who had commended him in the past fell silent, leaving him to face the full wrath of the liberal left. Most black and white Americans had never heard of John Ashcroft. However, they were immediately smothered in an avalanche of anti-Ashcroft demagoguery by the black establishment and their liberal allies.

When Gov. Jeb Bush, on his own volition, instituted a race-neutral program to protect college admissions and state contracting programs from constitutional attacks on racial preference grounds, black Florida lawmakers staged a '60s style sit-in and distorted the goals of the "One Florida Program." Meanwhile, the levels of minority contractors and college admissions have increased.

When President Bush appointed the first black secretary of state, the first female—and black—national security advisor, and a black secretary of education, those so-called leaders and their feminist and liberal allies directly or indirectly discounted such appointments. They would apparently rather have a white liberal than a black appointee who does not dance to their liberal tune.

Why do these overseers remain in positions of influence? They have powerful partners.

A major partner is the national media. With the exception of the Fox News Channel, few if any major networks and their affiliates have black guests or commentators on a regular basis who express contrasting political and philosophical views. Most of the producers seem to use the same "black leader" Rolodex. Hence, the viewing public rarely sees blacks with contrasting views. By limiting the diversity of viewpoint that does exist in the black community, such media outlets do a grave disservice to all Americans and unwittingly foster division and misunderstanding between the races.

For years, surveys of black Americans have reflected views opposite those of the black leadership on issues such as school choice, the death penalty, abortion and prayer in school. For example, as recently as last year, a poll by the Joint Center for Political and Economic Studies found that 57% of black Americans support school vouchers. Yet, we rarely see blacks in the media reflecting such views.

Most black journalists are another link in this partnership chain. Many share the same liberal viewpoints as most of the black leadership establishment. And even if there is disagreement, there appears to be reluctance on the part of most of them to openly question or criticize such leaders for fear of being ostracized for going against the civil rights chorus. Who wants to be called an "Uncle Tom" or a "tool" of white conservatives? How many black journalists who fumed over the "Willie Horton" ad criticized the NAACP for its race-baiting political ad against George W. Bush or raised questions about why so many new black voters in Florida were not educated on the ballot process? Few, if any.

Break the Monopoly

What can be done to break the "Soul Police" monopoly of the black leadership?

Black Americans must become responsible for their own political fate. No other group's votes are as discounted, cheap and taken for granted as are those of black Americans.

Both political parties seek out Jewish, Italian, blue-collar, elderly, Hispanic and white female voters. They are not taken for granted. A political strategist in 1979 could have generally predicted the black turnout for Republicans and Democrats in the presidential elections of '80, '84, '92, '96 and 2000. That is a recipe for political impotence.

Blacks must demonstrate political sophistication and diversity at the ballot box. Even though Hispanic voters gave 67% of their vote to Gore, 31% voted for Bush. Hence, their votes will be in play by both parties for years to come. If just 10% to 20% of blacks in those states with significant black populations were to register Republican and vote in GOP presidential and senatorial primaries, the whole tenor of the GOP—as well as the Democratic Party—would change. There would be an earthquake in both parties. Even though it would serve the best political interests of black America, it is unlikely that any of the present crop of "leaders" would advocate such a position. They are too attached to the umbilical cord of the Democratic liberal establishment.

It is also time for blacks to make their leaders accountable. The fact that Democratic Representatives Carrie Meek, Corrine Brown and Alcee Hastings—all from Florida—failed to attend the President's meeting with the Congressional Black Caucus should be cause for criticism from their black constituents and their local press. After complaining about the Florida election results and castigating the GOP for failure to reach out, they balked when their time came to meet with the President. Thousands of their black constituents had no representation in that meeting.

It was wise for the President to meet with the caucus. There should be no illusion, however, that the legislative Black Caucuses in Washington or Tallahassee will support many of the educational and social programs of either President Bush or Gov. Bush. Too many of their members will not do anything to alienate their Democratic allies—unions, pro-abortion feminists and others in the liberal coalition—to whom many look to help fill their fundraising coffers.

Meanwhile, the GOP and conservatives should stick to their principles, reach out to groups in the black community that share the same values on education and other issues, and undertake a continuing major campaign to educate black rank-and-file voters on their beliefs and their impact on the black community.

These values and beliefs were clearly set forth 21 years ago in the 1980 Republican Platform:

"Republicans will not make idle promises to blacks and other minorities; we are beyond the day when any American can live off rhetoric or political platitude.... Nor are we prepared to accept the practice of turning the poor into permanent wards of the state, trading their political support for continued financial assistance."

Will the "overseers" and their liberal allies keep their black flock behind the gates of the liberal plantation for the next 21 years? Or, will a new generation of black voters and leaders finally bring political emancipation?

© HUMAN EVENTS, 2001

Black Caucus Deceives Blacks on Trump

Tuesday, January 7, 2020 06:35 PM

It's really a shame how the once credible Congressional Black Caucus (CBC) has degenerated into being a puppet of the Democratic Party and its interests — not those of its black constituents.

The most recent example is the CBC's totally dishonest comments on the Trump administration. It's Dec. 19 press release, stated in part:

"Black people have lost a lot since President Trump was sworn into office. The list of regressive and racist policies proposed by Donald Trump's administration is long and sad. To add insult to injury . . . he has never championed a single policy or program for black people."

What an outright lie!

The CBC is being dishonest with its own black constituents.

Here are the facts:

On unemployment, the Trump economy has reduced the black unemployment rate to record lows averaging 5.4 percent over the past four months.

As to black women, the CBC obviously missed The Wall Street Journal Sept. 20 editorial stating that the greatest employment gains for full-time year-round workers in 2018 were among minority female-led households including a 4.2 percentage point increase among blacks. And, the poverty rate among female households declined 2.7 percentage points for blacks.

I guess the CBC would consider that a loss for blacks.

A Dec. 16, 2019, White House Fact Sheet outlined several accomplishments of the president's economic policies. These include the addition of more than seven million jobs; annual nominal wages growing by 3% last year for the first time in a decade; and, wage growth being higher for lower-income workers compared to higher-income workers, workers compared to managers and black Americans compared to white Americans.

The CBC would have us believe that none of these statistics benefit blacks.

As the saying goes, "a rising tide lifts all boats."

I guess to the CBC, this doesn't apply to blacks.

The liberal-leaning Brookings Institution, in an October Report, "Black Household Income is Rising Across the United States," found otherwise.

It should be required reading for the CBC.

Among the report's findings was that among the top five U.S. metropolitan areas with the largest black populations, there were significant increases in median black household incomes in the five-year period 2013-2018.

In the New York metro area, the increase was 14.6 percent, Atlanta 20.8 percent, Chicago 11.3 percent, Dallas 12.2 percent and Washington D.C. 7.1 percent.

The report also notes that the metro areas in the West and South recorded the largest statistically increases in black median household incomes.

What accounts for these positive changes?

The report said that one likely factor is "employment opportunity" and stated that there was a "positive, significant association between the change in black employment rates and black median household incomes across the metro areas from 2013 to 2018."

The CBC would have you believe that these increases in income and the decrease in unemployment of blacks is because Trump "inherited" Obama's economy.

What a joke!

There is no way the economic gains we have seen since the president came into office would have occurred with the Obama and the Democrats' tax, spend and regulate philosophy of government. The success we are experiencing is because of the president's — not Obama's — policies.

Trump's tax cuts continue to bring tax relief to American small businesses, thereby boosting disposable income for most households. His actions reducing the scope and cost of federal regulations have been an essential ingredient in the increase in new jobs, rising wages, and low unemployment.

I guess the CBC would call these policies "racist and regressive" and of no benefit to black Americans.

As to the CBC's allegation that the president "never" championed a "single policy or program for black people," it's obviously unaware that the president's 2020 budget request devoted significant resources to school choice programs to benefit low-income children trapped in failing inner city schools.

Do they think vouchers and school choice for poor students are "regressive and racist?"

I assume that the CBC would also consider the president's championing of the First Step Act and criminal justice reform to reduce sentences of thousands of prisoners and expand job training programs to decrease recidivism to be "regressive and racist" even though 91.3 percent of prisoners with reduced sentences were black.

Let's not forget the president's support and advocacy of Opportunity Zones to incentivize investment in low-income communities or increasing federal funding for Historically Black Colleges and Universities (HBCU) by more than $100 million over the last two years, a 17% increase since 2017.

Does the CBC consider these efforts to be "regressive and racist" and of no benefit to black people?

Barack Obama may have been the first president sharing the same skin color as his fellow black Americans and members of the CBC, however, it's Donald Trump whose economic and social policies benefit black Americans.

ABOUT THE AUTHOR

Clarence McKee is a *Newsmax.com* "Insider," where his extensive writings can be found on his "Silent Minority" Blog (www.Newsmax. com/mckee) and appeared on *Newsmax* TV's *America Talks Live* offering his political insights. His articles and commentary have been published in *Human Events Online, The Washington Times, The Tampa Tribune, The South Florida Sun-Sentinel,* and *Front Page Florida.com.* He is also a contributor to the *South Florida Sun-Sentinel's* "South Florida 100," commenting on local and national political issues.

McKee served on the US Senate staff for Senator Jacob K. Javits (R-NY) whom he assisted in writing food stamp and school lunch legislation and was a legal assistant at the Federal Communications Commission to Commissioner Benjamin L. Hooks—who later headed the NAACP—where he assisted in drafting Equal Employment Opportunity and Minority Ownership policies for the broadcasting and cable television industries.

He held a number of posts during the Reagan-Bush administrations, including serving on President-Elect Reagan's transition team, and was an appointee to the Legal Services Corporation board of directors. He gave political commentaries on WTTG-TV Television's *Ten O'Clock News* in Washington, D.C. and was a Registered Foreign Agent, media, and political relations advisor for the Angolan Freedom Fighters ("UNITA") in its efforts to defeat the Soviet-Cuban–backed Angolan government.

He is the former co-owner of WTVT-TV in Tampa; a former chairman of the Florida Association of Broadcasters; served on several corporate boards, including Barnett Banks, Inc. and Checkers Drive-In Restaurants; and was inducted into the Tampa Bay Business Hall of Fame.

McKee was appointed by Florida governors Jeb Bush and Charlie Crist to several boards and commissions and was a Florida delegate to the 2008 Republican National Convention. His Florida-based company provides government, political, media relations, and media training to clients.

He worked his way through college and law school in a variety of jobs, including being a railroad dining car waiter, bartender, and a disc jockey. He received his BA degree from Hobart College and his Doctor of Jurisprudence degree from the Howard University School of Law.

ENDNOTES

1 https://www.blackenterprise.com/
president-obama-interview-small-business-unemployment-exclusive/

2 https://www.huffpost.com/entry/
laura-ingraham-martin-luther-king-jr_n_5ca732bbe4b0a00f6d3e26c6

3 https://thehill.com/blogs/blog-briefing-room/news/182209-cbc-chair-man-if-obama-wasnt-in-office-we-would-be-marching-on-white-house

4 https://www.huffpost.com/entry/tavis-smiley-obama-black-wealth_n_5
69820dbe4b0ce496423f053

5 https://www.newsmax.com/Insiders/ClarenceVMcKee/id-150/

6 https://www.newsmax.com/clarencevmckee/
obama-gop-urban-agenda/2013/02/04/id/488864/

7 https://news.gallup.com/poll/194495/obama-effect-racial-matters-falls-short-hopes.aspx

8 https://www.npr.org/sections/itsallpolitics/2011/09/26/140802831/
obama-stop-complaining-order-to-cbc-fires-up-some-folks

9 https://www.npr.org/sections/itsallpolitics/2011/09/26/140802831/
obama-stop-complaining-order-to-cbc-fires-up-some-folks

10 https://www.huffpost.com/entry/maxine-waters_n_930712

11 https://www.rollcall.com/news/
new-cbc-chairman-black-america-is-in-a-state-of-emergency

12 http://www.crewof42.com/news/cbc114-butterfield-speech-text/

13 https://www.telegraph.co.uk/news/worldnews/baracko-
bama/11779946/Barack-Obama-has-done-zero-for-black-people.html

14 https://www.youtube.com/watch?v=tVhnUvQURP8

15 https://time.com/4630300/
tavis-smiley-obama-criticism-love/?xid=fbshare

16 https://www.foxnews.com/opinion/laura-ingraham-dems-return-to-
racial-pandering-and-grievance-peddling-and-sharptons-the-king-queen-
maker

17 https://www.whitehouse.gov/briefings-statements/president-donald-j-
trumps-efforts-combat-crisis-southern-border-delivering-results/

18 https://www.mediaite.com/online/nancy-pelosi-on-trumps-immigra-
tion-proposal-he-wants-to-make-america-white-again/

19 https://www.foxnews.com/media/
tom-homan-wasserman-schultz-white-supremacy-immigration

20 https://www.dailysignal.com/2018/06/26/
fact-check-are-half-of-all-border-patrol-agents-hispanic/

21 https://www.latimes.com/opinion/op-ed/la-oe-seminara-trump-immi-
gration-reform-african-americans-20180316-story.html?_amp=true

22 https://www.vox.com/2019/2/5/18212533/
president-trump-state-of-the-union-address-live-transcript

23 https://www.apnews.com/105e865eb42344688ee83cf50b2133f6

24 https://www.ussc.gov/sites/default/files/pdf/research-and-publications/retroactivity-analyses/first-step-act/201900607-First-Step-Act-Retro.pdf

25 https://www.apnews.com/105e865eb42344688ee83cf50b2133f6

26 https://www.prisonpolicy.org/reports/outofwork.html#fnref:13

27 https://www.vice.com/en_us/article/59ebex/president-obama-heads-to-prison-in-pursuit-of-criminal-justice-reform

28 https://noblenational.org/wp-content/uploads/2017/02/President-Barack-Obama-Task-Force-on-21st-Century-Policing-Implementation-Guide.pdf

29 https://obamawhitehouse.archives.gov/my-brothers-keeper

30 https://www.newsmax.com/dralvedacking/trump-abortion-prolife-national-crisis/2019/01/25/id/899858/

31 https://www.politico.com/story/2012/08/the-abortion-extremist-080013?o=1

32 https://www.realclearpolitics.com/video/2019/01/18/president_trump_speech_to_march_for_life.htm

33 https://www.vox.com/policy-and-politics/2019/2/5/18212521/state-of-the-union-trump-abortion-northam

34 https://www.wsj.com/articles/abortions-dred-scott-moment-11549583717

35 https://www.lifesitenews.com/opinion/democratic-party-celebrates-black-history-month-by-aborting-more-black-babi

36 https://youtu.be/t568Nd7k_Yk?t=624

37 https://www.dailysignal.com/2019/05/17/satisfaction-high-in-dc-school-voucher-program-study-finds/

38 https://www.usnews.com/opinion/blogs/peter-roff/2009/04/22/obama-wrong-on-dc-school-vouchers-and-hypocritical-just-like-congress

39 https://www.cnn.com/2009/POLITICS/03/11/martin.vouchers/index.html

40 https://www.investors.com/politics/editorials/obama-budget-leaves-every-child-behind/

41 https://www.washingtontimes.com/news/2015/feb/8/stephen-moore-obamas-budget-tries-to-kill-dc-schoo/

42 https://www.politico.com/tipsheets/morning-education/2017/05/trump-administration-reverses-obama-policy-on-dc-vouchers-220150

43 https://edsource.org/2019/trump-renews-call-for-school-choice-legislation-in-state-of-the-union-speech/608259

44 https://www2.ed.gov/about/overview/budget/budget20/summary/20summary.pdf#page=4

45 https://sites.ed.gov/freedom/

46 https://sites.ed.gov/freedom/category/fact-sheet/

47 https://www.federationforchildren.org/national-school-choice-poll-shows-67-of-voters-support-school-choice-2019/

48 https://www.newsmax.com/clarencevmckee/desantis-trump-presidential-election-school-choice/2018/11/27/id/892192/

49 https://www.wsj.com/articles/school-choice-moms-tipped-the-governors-florida-race-1542757880

50 https://www.wsj.com/articles/charter-schools-ace-another-test-11570143771

51 https://www.newsmax.com/clarencevmckee/obama-president-ferguson/2014/11/28/id/609959/

52 https://www.irs.gov/newsroom/opportunity-zones-frequently-asked-questions

53 https://www.whitehouse.gov/briefings-statements/president-donald-j-trump-lifting-american-communities-left-behind/

54 https://politico-money.simplecast.com/episodes/the-100-billion-question-a-conversation-cef792a3

55 https://www.whitehouse.gov/presidential-actions/executive-order-establishing-white-house-opportunity-revitalization-council/

56 https://www.hud.gov/sites/dfiles/Main/documents/WHORC-Implementation-Plan.pdf

57 https://www.cnbc.com/2019/09/12/robert-johnson-gives-trump-credit-for-doing-positive-things.html

58 https://www.bls.gov/news.release/empsit.nr0.htm

59 https://www.census.gov/library/publications/2019/demo/p60-266.html

60 https://fns-prod.azureedge.net/sites/default/files/resource-files/34SNAPmonthly-2.pdf

61 https://fns-prod.azureedge.net/sites/default/files/pd/SNAPsummary.pdf

62 https://fns-prod.azureedge.net/sites/default/files/ops/Characteristics2013.pdf

63 https://fns-prod.azureedge.net/sites/default/files/resource-files/Characteristics2017.pdf

64 https://www.cnn.com/2019/12/20/economy/trump-economy/index.html

65 https://www.brookings.edu/blog/the-avenue/2019/10/03/black-household-income-is-rising-across-the-united-states/

66 https://www.whitehouse.gov/briefings-statements/president-donald-j-trump-ensuring-forgotten-americans-forgotten-no/

67 https://www.cnbc.com/2019/12/31/dow-futures-last-trading-day-of-2019.html?__source=facebook%7Cmain

68 https://www.whitehouse.gov/briefings-statements/president-trumps-historic-deregulation-benefitting-americans/

69 https://thehill.com/blogs/blog-briefing-room/news/281936-obama-to-trump-what-magic-wand-do-you-have

70 https://www.whitehouse.gov/articles/two-years-tax-cuts-continue-boosting-united-states-economy/

71 https://www.newsmax.com/clarencevmckee/trump-congressional-black-caucus-naacp-jack-johnson/2018/06/13/id/865867/

72 https://cbc.house.gov/news/documentsingle.aspx?DocumentID=2123

73 https://thegrio.com/2009/10/09/all-eyes-are-on-rep/

74 https://www.realclearpolitics.com/video/2016/08/16/trump_the_democrats_have_taken_advantage_of_african-american_voters_i_will_rebuild_inner_cities.html